What Others Are Saying About
In Heavenly Arms

"Dr. Bridgman has written a singularly unique book on a topic far too often misunderstood. What an effective and healing work!"

— Christopher Hoffman, MD
ER Physician

"This book is long overdue to help those couples who in the past have suffered alone. Now they can find comfort and healing through In Heavenly Arms."

— Jene Wilson
Founder & Director
American Family Living

"In Heavenly Arms is an invaluable healing tool for guiding others through the grieving process."

— Richard & Karen Hacker
Empty Arms Group Facilitators

"This is the most sensitive, resourceful and helpful book I have ever read!"

— Syndie Kahl
Lay Counselor &
Former "Empty Arms" Support Group Member

In Heavenly Arms
Grieving The Loss & Healing The Wounds Of Miscarriage

In Heavenly Arms
Grieving The Loss & Healing The Wounds Of Miscarriage

by Shari L. Bridgman, Ph.D.

BLACKHAWK CANYON PUBLISHERS
LAGUNA HILLS, CA

Scripture taken from the HOLY BIBLE, NEW INTERNATIONAL VERSION. Copyright 1973, 1978, 1984 International Bible Society. Used by permission of Zondervan Bible Publishers.

Second Printing December 1999

The names of all persons in this book except for the author and her immediate family have been changed in the interest of privacy.

Library of Congress Cataloging-in-Publication Data
Bridgman, Shari, 1960-
        In Heavenly Arms: Grieving the loss and
    healing the wounds of miscarriage / by Shari
    Bridgman, Ph.D. —
         p.
    Includes bibliographical references
    ISBN 0-9657698-3-6 : $12.95
    1. Self-actualization/Self-help
    2. Psychology/Psychiatry
    3. Religion/Bibles
    4. Family/Child Care/Relationships
    5. Medical/Nursing/Home Care

Contents

ACKNOWLEDGMENTS

When I first decided to write this book, I naively underestimated the time and energy it would take. Writing a book while being a full-time mommy to two preschool boys was a challenging task. Frequently, I thought of shelving the book project. Yet God kept me going and sent me people along the way to nudge and encourage me.

More specifically, I thank my mother for her willingness to lend her expertise to this seemingly endless endeavor of mine. Her feedback and critique of my writing style renewed my motivation and passion for this book.

I thank my sister, Tracey, for reviewing my manuscript during her Christmas vacation from teaching! But most of all, I thank Tracey for her willingness to help me bear the pain of my losses. During two of my miscarriages, she dropped everything to drive two hours up the coast so that she could support me in person.

And with a grateful heart, I thank my husband, Laird, whose love, support, and tenderness were unfailing during my darkest hours of grief. He is truly one of the most compassionate people I have ever known. I am blessed to have the opportunity to love him and to be loved by him.

Laird also proved to be a gifted editor as I worked to complete this book — which has been through countless metamorphoses. I am incredibly grateful that during the long process of writing and rewriting, Laird was encouraging when I was discouraged and optimistic when I was pessimistic. I am also fortunate that he rescued computer-illiterate me from several near-death (mine) computer catastrophes!

This book is dedicated to
my precious babies,
Jared, Diandra, and Benjamin,
who rest in heavenly arms.

PREFACE

In 1990, after a year of trying to get pregnant, my husband and I lost the first child we had ever conceived. My miscarriage was a shattering experience. It plunged me into a torrent of different emotions — sadness, anger, rage, hurt, confusion — that I struggled to understand. Unfortunately, I found very little professional support tailored to the needs of Christian miscarriage survivors. Perhaps my doctor and my friends assumed that since I was a psychotherapist, I would be able to find the help I needed on my own, but I was in no shape to handle my own emotional needs. It is because of my experience that this book exists.

Although other people may minimize your loss by suggesting that your baby was simply an embryo, fetus, or fetal tissue, you know that your baby was real and that emotionally you were prepared to give birth to a baby, not a fetus. My hope is that this book will become a friend in your time of grief — something to turn to that lets you know someone understands your pain. The exercises in this book are designed specifically for you as a miscarriage survivor. Step by step you will be guided through your grieving process. Please know that you are not alone.

Shari L. Bridgman, Ph.D.
Laguna Hills, 1997

INTRODUCTION

If you have had a miscarriage, you have suffered a devastating loss. Your precious and beloved baby is gone and you may experience any or all of the following:

❖ Trouble being around babies

Malls, parks, nurseries, theme parks, and baby showers are places where you suffer in silent agony.

❖ Unrelenting depression and grief

You cry while watching a diaper commercial on television or while seeing a mother pushing a stroller. Laughter and joy seem a lifetime away.

❖ Intense anger at God

You wonder how a loving God could be so cruel as to let your baby die. Perhaps your miscarriage has even shaken your faith in God.

❖ A sense of isolation and despair

It seems as if no one understands your pain. You wonder how you can survive the loss of your innocent baby.

❖ Fear of trying to conceive again

Sex and intimacy have become emotional mine fields for you and your spouse. What was intended to be a beautiful expression of love is now a stressful, conflict-ridden experience.

If any or all of these effects describe you, you are not alone. These facets of grief are common and natural responses to the death of your baby. It is also common for people to try to stuff or ignore their pain. After all, well-intentioned friends and relatives may reassure you that "time heals all wounds." Unfortunately, this is not entirely true. If you push your feelings down and hide from your tragic loss, the repressed pain will become like emotional poison to you — seeping out in unexpected and damaging ways. However, the GOOD NEWS is that there is HOPE for healing your emotional wounds.

This book will help you:

❖ Acknowledge your feelings

True healing and acceptance of your loss begin as you use your feelings to help you understand your grieving process.

❖ Appropriately express your anger

Your anger is an indicator that something is wrong and you are hurting inside. When you make anger your ally, you can begin to heal your pain.

❖ Enhance your communication and intimacy with your spouse

Tragically, miscarriages can cause painful rifts in marriages. Learn how to avoid this by practicing healthy sharing and listening techniques.

❖ Say goodbye to your precious baby

Learn to say goodbye in a special way, secure in the knowledge that your precious child is now living with Jesus. Letting go is necessary for you to move on with your life.

❖ Find peace about your loss

As you acknowledge your pain, express your feelings, let go of your baby, and claim God's promises, you will be more fully able to accept God's peace.

Chapter One

SHATTERED DREAMS

*"Nothing seems so tragic to one who is old
as the death of one who is young, and this alone
proves that life is a good thing."*

— Zoe Akins

The stick was blue! A very, very pale blue — but undeniably blue! And I was ecstatic. Quickly, I scrambled around the house to make sure that every detail of the moment perfectly replicated the dream I had envisioned countless times. Quietly slipping into my favorite summer dress, I put on a splash of makeup and fussed with my hair. Next, I rushed from cupboards to pantry to refrigerator until I was holding a breakfast tray stacked with fruit, muffins, cereal, and juice. Tiptoeing down the hall to our bedroom, I gently coaxed awake my sleeping husband, Laird.

I waited for Laird to finish breakfast, tapping my foot against the nightstand and watching him chew each spoonful of cereal and swallow every sip of orange juice. An eternity seemed to pass then, finally, Laird pushed his empty tray away, kissed my cheek, and smiled contentedly. "Wow, that was great. What's the occasion?" he asked as he patted his rather full stomach.

Grinning mischievously, I presented him with the special card that I had been saving for just such an occasion. "HAPPY FATHER'S DAY," it read. Then I handed him the blue stick from the home pregnancy test I had just taken. "Really?" he asked incredulously. "Are you sure? Could this really be happening?" We hugged, we laughed, we cried, and we even jumped up and down on the bed. After a long and discouraging year of trying to conceive a child, I was finally pregnant!

Actually, to describe that past year as discouraging is a huge understatement. Anyone who has tried unsuccessfully to conceive understands the heartache that Laird and I endured. Each month a small seed of hope would sprout. "Maybe it's this month. I'm feeling some strange twinges. Is that nausea? Something's different this time, I know it." When my period would start, I would once again withdraw into my cave of despair, not wanting to go anywhere or do anything. As I hid inside our small, dark condo, ruminating doubts hovered over me. "What did we do wrong? We probably missed my ovulation date again. Maybe there's something wrong with my body and I'll never be able to conceive. I'll probably never be a mother. Maybe I wouldn't even make a good mother and God is protecting some poor, defenseless child from me."

Eventually, I became so baby-sensitive that I couldn't even watch a diaper commercial on television without crying. It seemed as if pregnant women were invading our neighborhood, too. Everywhere I went I was confronted with the large bellies and glowing faces of what I perceived to be blissfully happy pregnant women! To make it even harder to cope, many of our close friends were into their second pregnancies during this time and the tick of my biological clock was resonating loudly inside my head. My arms ached to cradle a baby, yet God seemed to be saying no. I was angry and despondent because I couldn't understand why God would deny us our own baby.

And now here we were hugging and shouting for joy because we were finally pregnant! All of a sudden the agony and desperation of the last year simply vanished. Gleefully, I threw away the phone number of a local fertility specialist, thankful that we would not need his expertise. Then I rushed to the phone to call my best friend who was three months pregnant herself. She was thrilled and we were both very excited about experiencing our first pregnancies together.

Soon I was choosing my obstetrician and visiting her for the first time. We chatted amiably in her designer decorated office splashed in watercolor pastels and generously filled with beautiful plants. The experience was exciting and surreal at the same time — was I truly pregnant? After our discussion and my exam, the doctor gave me a packet stuffed with pamphlets, coupons, and free samples — it was like Christmas for a first time mom. I repeatedly sifted through this neonatal care package in the next few weeks, reading every scrap of paper and dreaming about how wonderful it would be to use the itty-bitty diaper sample on my own sweet baby.

On the way home from my doctor's office after this first visit, I couldn't resist the temptation to indulge my mommy-to-be cravings. Stopping by the neighborhood mall, I wandered into the toy stores, shaking baby rattles, and squeezing stuffed animals to determine whether or not they would be soft and cuddly enough for my precious baby. I browsed through the baby clothes in the department stores, envisioning my beautiful baby snuggling in fuzzy, warm sleepers and crawling in multicolored jumpsuits. I even stopped to try on several maternity outfits, imagining proudly how I would be filling them out in a few months.

As the next few weeks passed by, however, I was a little bit bothered because I did not have any of the typical signs of pregnancy. No nausea, no added fatigue, and no increased sensitivity to odors or particular foods. I was only mildly concerned though, concluding that I must be one of the "lucky" ones. After all, my best friend was into her second trimester and she had experienced only a few days of mild nausea. In retrospect I know the absence of pregnancy symptoms is not usually a good sign.

Ten weeks into my pregnancy I awoke one morning with a vague sense of foreboding. My apprehension escalated when I discovered that I was spotting. "I'm not bleeding a lot, maybe it's nothing," I tried to reassure myself, longing for it to be nothing. "Besides," I reasoned silently, "God wouldn't let anything happen to our baby. He knows how much we want a child."

The harder I tried to convince myself that nothing was wrong, the more my anxiety skyrocketed. After watching me pace around the living room, talking aloud to no one in particular, Laird finally announced, "This whole pregnancy thing is new to us. I don't know if your spotting is anything to worry about, but let's just call the doctor and get her opinion." Calmed by Laird's decisiveness, I phoned the doctor only to find that she was not in that day. The receptionist spoke in a cheerful voice, however, and promised that the nurse practitioner would return my call. After hanging up the phone, I felt certain that the nurse would call soon so, for a long time, I stared at the kitchen phone, willing it to ring. Only silence greeted me.

"Why don't you try to eat something?" Laird suggested, aware that I had neglected my breakfast.

I stood in front of the open refrigerator for several minutes while cold air chilled my arms and legs. Why was it open? I couldn't remember. Throughout the next several hours, I made frequent trips to the bathroom to see if the spotting had either stopped or increased, while Laird sat silently on the couch aimlessly clicking the television remote control. Eventually, Laird concluded that we had been patient long enough. He grabbed the phone and dialed the doctor's office, insisting, in his no-nonsense voice, to speak with an available doctor immediately. After a few minutes of conversation, he hung up the receiver and announced, "Let's get ready. One of the other doctors at the office has scheduled an ultrasound for you at the hospital in thirty minutes!"

Grabbing my wallet, I forced down eight ounces of water before we got into the car. I followed the doctor's instructions and gulped the remaining 24 ounces of water in the course of the twenty minute drive to the hospital. As luck would have it, we then had to wait over an hour past our scheduled appointment time before the nurse escorted me back to radiology! There I had sat with a bladder seemingly stretched to the size of a basketball, tightly crossing my legs, trying not to move, waiting... and waiting... and waiting. At the time, this hour of "water torture" in the hospital lobby was not particularly amusing. Later, however, it proved to be our only source of humor during the next dark hours.

Surviving my bulging bladder without any embarrassing incidents was a great relief. Eventually, we were directed to the ultrasound room where I put on an threadbare hospital gown and met the technician. She asked me a few questions; otherwise, she was very quiet — too quiet. Repeatedly she moved her instrument over the same place on my stomach as if she were looking for something she couldn't find. I could see the monitor from where I lay, but I had never had an ultrasound before and I could not decipher the various shapes and shadings on the screen. "So what's the verdict?" I asked expectantly. Expressionless, she answered, "I am only authorized to perform the ultrasound. The results will be sent to your doctor and she will review them with you."

My heart sank. I suspected that if the news were good, the technician would have let something slip. She gave me no indication of hope. No smile, no "Don't worry," no "It'll be okay." Laird and I were simply sent home to wait for our doctor's appointment scheduled later that afternoon.

During the day, I tried unsuccessfully to keep occupied with laundry, ironing, and emptying the dishwasher. Most of the time, however, I just wandered up and down our small hallway, repeatedly checking the bedroom clock to see whether it was time to leave for the doctor's office. Laird tinkered around on his computer and eventually played some James Taylor songs on the stereo to try to calm me. Neither one of us spoke much as the weight of not knowing descended upon us.

Several hours later as we sat in the examination room, the doctor was cautiously noncommittal about the sonogram results. "It doesn't show any evidence of an embryonic yolk sac, but that could be because the pregnancy is in an earlier stage than we originally thought. You aren't really bleeding very much and your cervix is closed — which are good signs. At this point, all we can do is wait to see what your body is going to do. If you are going to miscarry, there is really nothing that we can do to prevent it. I recommend that you go home and put your feet up."

With that recommendation, she sent us home with pamphlets about miscarriage and ectopic pregnancy. As we drove towards our condo, I read the warning signs for an ectopic pregnancy and the knot in my stomach tightened. Suddenly, it was hard for me to breathe. "Oh great," I said to Laird, trying to disguise my fear in sarcasm. "Not only could our baby die, but if the pregnancy's ectopic, I could die, too!" Laird didn't say anything but he reached over and squeezed my hand. His normally crystal blue eyes were clouded with alarm.

Once home, I tried to put my feet up as the doctor had suggested. Laird positioned pillows under my feet and my head until I was comfortable. He brought me some water to drink; he microwaved a TV dinner; he coaxed me to eat something. I picked at the food on my dinner tray for a few minutes, making designs in the mashed potatoes and squashing the peas with my fork. But I had no appetite. Exhausted, I just wanted to go to sleep and forget the whole miserable day ever began. Instead I found I couldn't lie still and I started tossing, turning, and thrashing at my sheets. Eventually, I gave up on the idea of resting and joined Laird in the living room.

Together we sat on our sofa, held hands, and prayed for God's mercy and protection. Silently, I pleaded with God for the life of my baby. I remember trying to recall Bible verses to reassure me that God would save our baby and this whole nightmare would have a happy ending. For a while it seemed as if a vacuum had simply sucked out all of my memory and no Scripture came to my mind.

Finally, I heard Psalm 37:4 repeating in my mind "Delight yourself in the Lord and He will give you the desires of your heart." "Yeah, right," I thought. "Just how in the world do I find 'delight' when my baby may be dying?" As I questioned God in my mind, painful twinges seized my abdomen.

"How bad is it? What should I do? Should we call the doctor?" Laird asked frantically. He wanted desperately to alleviate my pain and to prevent what we both knew in our hearts was happening.

The pain from the cramps was bearable, so I did not need further medical attention. All we could do was wait.

I sat on the sofa, cradled in Laird's arms, watching mean-ingless images flit across the television screen. A few hours later I passed some tissue and a warm, sickening feeling swept through my body. Standing in the bathroom, I couldn't believe that what I was looking at were the re-mains of my baby. Wanting so badly to be mistaken, I called Laird in to take a look, at the same time dreading what he would conclude. I waited in the living room while he examined the tissue. When he returned, his somber expression confirmed my worst fears: The baby that we had conceived in love to live a long and beautiful life was dead.

Chapter Two

THE EMOTIONAL HURRICANE

*"Out of defeat can come the best in human nature.
As Christians face storms of adversity, they may
rise with more beauty. They are like trees that
grow on mountain ridges — battered by winds, yet
trees in which we find the strongest wood."*

— Billy Graham

ur baby's death plunged me into a turbulent emotional hurricane. There were many times I felt desolate inside, as if someone had ripped me open and sucked everything out. I rarely smiled and I seldom laughed. "I miss that sparkle in your eyes," Laird murmured in concern, troubled that I remained emotionally unreachable. My cave became a familiar, yet cold, retreat from the harsh reality of the death of my baby and even the promise of my favorite things could not tempt me to venture from its darkness.

"Let's go hiking," Laird coaxed. "How would you like to drive up to the mountains? Would you like to go to the beach? What about a double scoop of chunky chocolate ice cream?"

27

I just looked at him and shrugged. "I don't really feel like it right now. Maybe later," I said indifferently.

The days dragged on as I was battered by this overpowering storm of grief. Many mornings I lay in bed trying to will my seemingly paralyzed body to get up and keep going. Other times I would discover that my mouth was moving and that sound was coming out, yet I didn't have any awareness of meaningful conversation! I somehow continued the routine of my life, but those first few weeks after my loss were a haze.

Any parent who has suffered the loss of a baby knows intimately this emotional hurricane. Sometimes your feelings may catch you unaware and latch onto you with unexpected tenacity. The resulting emotional unpredictability may be disruptive, frightening, or even embarrassing at times. (I used to burst into tears without warning.) On other occasions you may feel weary, despondent, and alone. My hope is that you will find that, in reality, you are NOT alone. I was both amazed and comforted to find so many miscarriage survivors around me. Remarkably, it seemed that everybody I knew had either experienced a miscarriage or knew a friend or family member who had suffered one. Each time I spoke with a fellow miscarriage survivor I felt understood and supported. Years later when Amy shared with me her journey into her own emotional hurricane, it sounded very familiar.

> *I'm such a mess. I cry when I see a diaper commercial on television and I can't even walk through the baby clothes section of a department store because I know I'll lose it. Yesterday I got angry when I found out one of my friends from college is pregnant. Can you believe it? I guess I felt a little jealous...it just doesn't seem fair...*

Amy had come to see me because she was distressed by her emotional experiences. I, too, remember being stunned and overwhelmed by the intensity of my feelings and reactions. Although, my professional training told me that this upheaval was a natural, normal reaction to my loss, I needed regular reassurance from other miscarriage survivors that I was not going crazy and that my life would return to normal.

THE GRIEF CYCLE

What Amy and I experienced were the various emotions that are a normal part of the grieving process. You, too, will experience similar feelings as you journey toward healing — and probably none of those feelings will seem the least bit normal! However, let me reassure you that the stages of the grief cycle are not only *normal* responses to a tragic loss, but they are also *necessary* responses. If you do not allow appropriate expression and understanding of your grief, you cannot begin to heal.

The following five stages of the grief cycle were observed by Elizabeth Kübler-Ross, MD as she worked extensively with terminally ill patients. Dr. Kübler-Ross discovered that although her patients' particular circumstances contained unique elements, the emotional journey they took to cope with their impending death and the grief resulting from this inevitability yielded remarkably consistent and similar paths. These stages of grief can be used as a basic road map to help you find your way as you journey through your pain. In particular, knowledge of these stages will help you understand what is happening to you emotionally and such understanding can often alleviate anxiety and fear. Do not be alarmed if you find yourself back at a stage you thought you had left behind. Traveling though the grief process often takes unexpected turns and circuitous routes. For example, the anniversary of your baby's death and your expected due date, as well as holidays and family reunions can temporarily reactivate certain phases of grief.

STAGE I

Denial — "This can't be happening to me."

Denial often occurs during the process of physically losing your baby as it did for me. During the time that I was spotting and cramping, I was trying desperately to minimize the potential seriousness of my symptoms. This denial stemmed from my emotional shock and my unwillingness to acknowledge the very painful reality that I was losing my baby. I reasoned, "This can't be happening. God knows how much we want a child. He gave this baby to us. Surely, He would never be so cruel as to take him away now." I had a white-knuckle grip on my fantasy that everything would be okay and I had a limited human understanding of God's plan for my future.

During the denial phase, your mind may also resort to what I call creative logic — it distorts and reshapes reality to fit your happily-ever-after fantasy. I remember my own creative logic had me telling myself, "I can't be having a miscarriage, I don't know anything about them." For a short period of time, I even felt relief as I reasoned with myself using this faulty thinking. Of course I was jolted back to reality when I discovered that I could be totally ignorant about miscarriages and still experience one!

A second type of denial that occurs after a miscarriage is a denial of the significance of the intense personal nature of the loss. Several years ago I conducted a seminar on the aftermath of miscarriage during which I spoke to a number of grieving parents — many of them unaware at the time of the depth and pervasiveness of their grief.

One man approached me after I had finished speaking to ask me a few questions and share his thoughts with me.

> *I am a Viet Nam vet. It's not like I don't know about death. I had friends die in my arms. I saw babies die in Nam. I don't like to talk about the miscarriage with anyone — not even my wife. I don't understand why this is so hard.*

This death was so hard because this man lost his **son**. I do not mean in any way to minimize the deaths of the other people in his life. However this man, as many other parents who lose a child through miscarriage, was unaware of how deeply bonded he was to his unborn child. He had already formed images in his mind about his child's appearance. He had dreams about what his child would be like, what they would do together, and what kind of relationship they would have. You, too, had these dreams about your baby which is why your grief is so intense.

A third type of denial that is prevalent with miscarriage survivors is a denial or minimization of the feelings that accompany the loss. I have heard a number of different things from grieving parents that indicate they are trying to ignore their feelings — push them out of the way so they can get on with life. Some of the most common denials I have heard over the years include the following:

> *It's really no big deal. I mean, the pregnancy was an accident anyway. I cried a little, but now it's over.*

> *I feel sad most of the time, but I can't give into it. I have a husband and other kids to take care of. I can't let them see me crying and depressed.*

*How can I complain? There are
people in the world suffering a lot worse
than I am.*

*If I let myself think about it, I'm afraid
I won't get anything done.*

*I can't cry forever. It's time to move
on.*

*It was sad, but we'll have another one
so I'm not going to think about this anymore. I don't want to dwell on the negative. That's not good for me.*

Do any of these comments sound familiar? If so, you
may be trying to deny your feelings and the significance
of your miscarriage. Undeniably, there comes a point in
time when you must choose to leave your sorrow behind
and move forward with your life. But, if you leap ahead
to this point without actually experiencing any of the healing your grieving process can bring, you will find yourself
paying for this avoidance in the future. Despite the fact
that your feelings are painful, it is important for your healing process that you work to break through your denial.
Keep in mind that while denial freezes your feelings in an
attempt to shelter you from pain, it also keeps you immobi-
lized. If you cannot move past your denial, you cannot
truly heal. The illusion of living a pain free life of denial
will shatter eventually.

STAGE II

*Anger — "What kind of God would allow an innocent
baby to die?"*

When Laird silently confirmed my fear that our baby
was dead, I felt gut wrenching anguish. I remember standing in my living room, fists raised in anger, raging at God.

"How could You do this? We trusted You! We prayed for mercy... for a healthy baby. Where were You? Why us? Why now? WHY?"

Anger often occurs when you cannot make sense of your loss. The death of our baby made absolutely no sense to me. It did not fit MY plan for my future. And for a time, I was unwilling to consider that there could be any plan for my life other than the one I had envisioned. Many people have similar feelings of anger towards God. They feel unfairly singled out, betrayed, or abandoned by a Heavenly Father who promised never to leave them. Oftentimes, God is not the only object of a miscarriage survivor's anger. Some people are angry at their doctor, their spouse, their pregnant friend, their family members, or even themselves.

While anger is a natural part of the grieving process, it is also a feeling that emotionally imprisons many people. Whenever I speak in public about grief recovery, I always caution people about the anger phase. First, it is imperative to find appropriate ways to express your anger because unchecked anger can be very destructive and hurtful to you and to others. Second, unresolved anger can easily turn to bitterness, and bitterness is like an insidious poison that taints your whole emotional system.

Once when I was a guest on a local talk radio show, I took a phone call from a woman named Nancy. Nancy was a tragic example of someone who had allowed her anger at her doctor and her hospital to turn into bitterness. As she shared the details of her story, it became clear that during the past five years Nancy had continued to blame her doctor and her hospital for her miscarriage, complaining bitterly that they had been unsympathetic. Nancy truly believed that her miscarriage could have been prevented if she had received competent, timely medical help. Instead of asking questions and investigating the plausibility of her claim that her miscarriage could have been avoided and then trying to work through her feelings, Nancy had chosen to immerse herself in her anger and resentment. She had been unable to move past this stage of her grief and, consequently, she had become bitter towards the medical community in general. Nancy was stuck. Her griping was not productive or cathartic — rather her complaining continued to fuel her bitterness and keep her from truly healing. This bitterness typically compounds the tragedy of a person's initial loss because it inevitably permeates other aspects of an individual's life, negatively affecting relationships with family, friends, and God.

STAGE III

Bargaining — "Please God, let my baby live. I promise I'll live a better life."

Bargaining usually involves a desperate plea from an anguished parent typically directed toward God. A parent hopes to convince God to save his or her child in exchange for payment of some type. When I was in this phase of grief, I truly believed that if God heard my impassioned prayers for mercy, that He would see things from my perspective. And it seemed only logical to conclude that He would then choose my bargain because it made perfect sense (to me).

I do believe that God fully and intimately understands our grief. I have no doubt that He understood my motivation for asking for deliverance for our baby since He is no stranger to grief. He loved us so much that He willingly sent His only Son to earth with full knowledge of the torment that Jesus would have to endure. And Christ accepted His fate even predicting His own suffering while He was here on earth.

> He [Jesus] then began to teach them that
> the Son of Man must suffer many things and
> be rejected by elders, chief priests, and
> teachers of the law, and that he must be
> killed and after three days rise again.
>
> Mark 8:31

Yes, God understood my pain. What I had failed to remember in my time of grief is that God has a COMPREHENSIVE PLAN and that my plan may not fit His. While God asks us to pray, He doesn't bargain. He does promise to listen to our prayers, search our hearts, and answer us according to His GOOD plan for our lives.

> For I know the plans I have for you, de-
> clares the Lord. Plans to prosper you and
> not to harm you. Plans to give you hope
> and a future.
>
> Jeremiah 29:11

> And we know that in all things God
> works for the good of those who love Him,
> who have been called according to His pur-
> pose.
>
> Romans 8:28

Sometimes our own grief and our inability to imagine any outcome other than the one for which we hope and pray cause us to misinterpret Scripture. Billie was also familiar with Jeremiah 29:11 — it was one of her favorite Bible verses. Her interpretation of it, along with other verses, had convinced her that God would save her unborn baby who had been diagnosed with an inevitably fatal chromosomal defect. Billie shared with me how she promised God that she and her husband would go to church every week, that they would tithe regularly, and that she would give up smoking if God would just let her baby live. God chose to allow Billie's baby to die. It was a shattering loss for her and she struggled for many months before she could accept that a loving God could allow an innocent baby to die.

STAGE IV

Depression — "I don't care about anything anymore. I just want to crawl into a hole and die."

Many miscarriage survivors report feelings of profound sadness, apathy, crying, insomnia, loss of appetite, and decreased energy. My own depression was overwhelming at times. I had intense feelings of hopelessness and I despaired that I would never conceive and give birth to a healthy baby. I cried often and I found it difficult to muster enthusiasm for dinner and a movie, a hike, or a night out with friends. It was especially hard to bounce back because it had taken us so long to get pregnant, because my biological clock was ticking loudly, and because I continued to watch my best friend's stomach swell as her pregnancy advanced without the slightest complication.

It is easy to get lost in this phase of the grief cycle, especially if you allow your grief to evolve into self-pity or a general attitude of apathy towards life. Lucy and Roger found their marriage suffering as Lucy's depression turned into a sour attitude about everything. Roger was the first to share during our session together.

> *I'm so sick of seeing Lucy just dragging through the day. Half the time she doesn't even get out of her pajamas. She doesn't care how she looks and she doesn't even try to get out and have fun. She certainly doesn't act like she cares about me anymore. Losing the baby was hard on me, too. But*

it's been six months and Lucy acts like she doesn't care about life anymore. I want my wife back!

Lucy responded to Roger's complaints with angry frustration:

I LOST A BABY!! You weren't the one who had all the morning sickness. You weren't the one who had to go through surgery because the baby was dead. I've been through a lot and I have a right to be depressed. Anyone knows that when you're depressed you don't feel like doing a lot of things.

Unfortunately, Lucy was using her miscarriage to justify and excuse her current inappropriate behavior. Her loss was undeniably tragic and painful. And, yes, depression is a normal part of the grieving process. But, when depression turns to self-pity, imprisons you in your grief, and even causes you to act unlovingly towards your family members, this is an unhealthy response to your loss. If you recognize yourself in Lucy's story, it is a good time to seek professional help just as Lucy and Roger did. Although it was a little frightening for them to make that initial phone call to schedule an appointment, they both agree that it was the right decision. Lucy and Roger worked hard in session, and over those next several weeks Lucy was able to differentiate between appropriate expression of her grief and the unhealthy self-pity in which she had been indulging. She saw how she was wallowing in her pain and ignoring herself, her husband, and other important relationships. Together we worked on the exercises in this book and Lucy made a conscious choice to recognize and to enjoy the good things in her life.

STAGE V

Acceptance — "I still feel pain about the death of my child, but I accept the reality of my loss and I am ready to go on with life."

Gloria knew that we were going to be saying goodbye to our babies in a special ceremony that is a part of our Empty Arms support group. She telephoned me prior to that meeting to express her discomfort with the idea of saying goodbye.

> *I really don't want to do this because I don't want to forget my baby. And anyway, I'm not sure that I'm ready because I still feel sad about losing her.*

As we talked, it became clear that, in spite of her concerns, Gloria really had progressed quite a bit through her grieving process and that she understood the significance and reality of her loss. She knew she could not change what had happened — that her baby really was gone. And she also knew it was normal and okay to feel sadness about her baby's death. I explained that saying goodbye did not mean that she must erase the memory of her baby from her mind and never think about her again. I also gave her permission not to participate in the goodbye ceremony if she still felt opposed to the concept after our phone conversation. I shared with her what it felt like for me when I came to terms with my loss. I told Gloria that I still feel a vague sense of emptiness and I miss not knowing my child. (I believe that he is waiting for me in heaven and that we will have eternity to become acquainted!) I shared with her that I had confronted my feelings about my miscarriage and had dealt with my fears about the future — "Would I get pregnant again? Would I have another miscarriage? Would I ever be a mother?"

I also explained to Gloria that a dull kind of sadness at the memory of my loss and what "could have been" remains with me. Fortunately, my sadness does not preoccupy my life because I have chosen to live in the present and to appreciate the abundant and undeserved blessings that I do have.

It was a healing telephone conversation for both of us. I discovered that helping Gloria in her grief recovery pointed out to me how far I had already journeyed in my own healing process and revealed to me new things about myself and God. And, as a result of our discussion, Gloria felt comforted and encouraged and ready to participate in the goodbye ceremony for her lost baby.

Chapter Three

MEMORIES

*"Grief fills the room up of my absent child,
lies in his bed, walks up and down with me,
puts on his pretty looks, repeats his words,
remembers me of all his gracious parts,
stuffs out his vacant garments with his form."*

— William Shakespeare

ach of you has memories that can lift your spirits,
restore your hope when you are in the midst of despair, and generally leave you with warm and peaceful feelings. You may fondly remember skipping stones across a lake during summer vacations, snitching a handful of your grandmother's freshly baked chocolate chip cookies, driving a car without your father's supervision, or walking down the aisle on your magical wedding day. It is easy to understand how positive memories such as these can be healing and most people will gladly recall happy events in their lives.

However, ask someone to remember something painful, traumatic, frightening, or sad, and the response is often markedly different. You may not believe it right now, but even the memories surrounding your miscarriage are powerful healing tools. They can help break through the brick wall that is guarding your heart and interfering with your natural grief process. As I struggled to find my own path through my grief, I discovered that after an initial period of withdrawal, I *wanted* to talk about my experiences. In fact, I found it was very beneficial to talk about even the more graphic physical aspects of my loss since these things had all added to my trauma. Recounting the details of my miscarriage promoted access to my feelings and also aided me in diffusing the emotional shock I had suffered.

Still, you may be asking, "Why do I have to relive my miscarriage? I've experienced enough pain. I don't want any **more** hurt." Such hesitancy and apprehension are natural responses and I remember Gary struggling with these questions when he and his wife scheduled an appointment for grief counseling.

Gary and Susan came to see me after their first miscarriage. As Susan recounted the painful events of their loss, silent tears streamed down her face and her hands trembled in her lap. Clearly her grief was intense and easily observable. When it was Gary's turn to share, he was brief.

> *I'm just here for Susan. I've been trying to tell her that she just needs to forget about this and move on. We can try again. I think that coming here [to counseling] to dwell on the pain will just make things worse for her.*

Gary's reactions to their miscarriage and to his wife's grief are common. Gary was in denial (remember the grief cycle?) about his own feelings concerning their loss and, because of this, he was having a difficult time understanding and accepting his wife's reaction. He really did believe that it was in Susan's best interest to "forget and move on" and, initially, he was a little suspicious of me. I deduced that he was trying to protect his wife from more hurt and felt wary of my intrusion into their private lives. (Fortunately, we were able to allay his concerns in this area early in the counseling process and continue productive work together.)

Many people share Gary's misperception that dealing with the memories of their miscarriage will cause additional pain. And who wants to endure more misery? You can be reassured that *remembering the details of your miscarriage does not create new pain*. Instead, this process simply allows the existing pain to come to the surface of your awareness. As agonizing as your memories may be, it is necessary for your pain to be a part of your conscious awareness so that you can then acknowledge it, understand it, and let go of it. Do not be deceived by the belief that if you ignore your pain, it will go away eventually. This can be a dangerous assumption. I have seen people in my counseling practice suffering from physical ailments, depression, anxiety, intense anger, and marital conflicts because they chose **not** to deal with various traumas in their lives. Denying your painful memories, does **not** make the pain magically disappear. It simply redirects the pain to find another means of expression — inevitably one that causes new forms of suffering.

You can choose a path other than denial. The following four exercises will help you use your memories to begin the healing process by penetrating that wall of denial and leading you to your true feelings. After you have completed these first four exercises, you are ready to tackle the next step in your healing journey. You must learn to identify your feelings — to name them. EXERCISES 5 and 6 will help you with this process. Identifying your feelings is important because it can help you make sense of your emotional chaos and give you clues as to which areas most need your healing efforts.

TIP: One of the best ways to take advantage of the healing exercises in this book is to purchase a three ring binder and create your own **Grief Recovery Notebook** (GRN). As you complete each exercise, your work can be included in this notebook so that you can review and reflect on your healing journey.

EXERCISE 1: Remembering Your Miscarriage

The second session of the Empty Arms support group that I lead can be emotionally painful, but it is also critically important. During this session I ask each person to share his or her miscarriage experience with the rest of the group using as much detail as time will permit. As you can imagine, this is difficult for a lot of people. But this kind of sharing also relieves a great burden for each miscarriage survivor and helps bond the group together. Now you, too, will use your memories of your miscarriage to help you begin the healing process.

On a separate piece of paper, answer the following questions with as much detail as you can recall and include your answers in your GRN.

- ❖ Date, time, and place of miscarriage?

- ❖ People present?

- ❖ Age of your baby?

- ❖ Describe your physical symptoms.

- ❖ Describe any significant involvement by medical professionals (positive or negative).

- ❖ Describe what happened.

- ❖ Did you see your baby? If yes, describe him/ her (some women see fetal tissue while others actually see the shape of a fetus or baby).

❖ What did you do/say after losing your baby?

❖ What did your spouse do/say after learning
of your miscarriage?

❖ What did other family members do/say after
learning of your miscarriage?

❖ What did your friends do/say after learning
of your miscarriage?

❖ Describe any other details that had an impact
on you.

EXERCISE 2: Sharing With a Safe Person

Sharing your story with a safe person is an important
step in your healing process. A safe person is someone
you can trust to listen to you without judgment, criticism,
or unsolicited advice. Someone who will offer prayer support and commit to praying for you on a regular basis as
you heal your pain. You should be able to trust this person to keep your confidence and should feel certain that
she will not try to preach at you or fix it so that you do not
feel any pain.

When you find a safe person, ask if you can talk with
her about your miscarriage experience. Explain that you
just need her to listen with understanding and empathy.
Share as much as you can about your feelings and your
loss.

EXERCISE 3: Sharing In a Support Group

If you are not already involved in a support group for
bereaved parents, consider joining one. Typically, a support group provides an excellent opportunity for parents
to share in a safe and supportive environment for free or
minimal cost to participants. (You can refer to the ap-

pendices on SELF-HELP ORGANIZATIONS and
ONLINE SUPPORT for assistance in selecting a group.
Also, your obstetrician or local hospital should have referrals for you — just ask.) Our Empty Arms support
group is designed specifically for the needs of parents suffering from the loss of a baby through miscarriage, stillbirth, or infant death. In our group, parents use the exercises in this book to facilitate their sharing and their healing process. Although most people find sharing to be a
draining experience, they are also relieved to find other
parents who have gone through similar losses and who
are feeling similar emotions.

EXERCISE 4: Healing Through Journaling

Writing down your thoughts, feelings, prayers, hopes,
and dreams in a journal can also be very healing. I often
assign journal writing to my counseling clients since it is
the type of exercise that can be cathartic and useful in a
wide variety of situations. Some people find it helpful to
write to the journal as if it were a good friend; others write
as if they were speaking to God. Consider journaling your
feelings and including these in your GRN.

EXERCISE 5: Identifying Your Feelings

Are you stumbling around aimlessly in your grief journey, feeling battered and tossed around by your unpredictable emotions? Sometimes a miscarrriage survivor's
emotions will come and go in such a flurry that decipher-
ing them seems impossible. If it feels like this to you, it
may be because you cannot slow down enough to focus.
The following exercise is structured to help you emotionally focus as you identify your feelings with words. Before
you begin this exercise, find a quiet place where you can
be assured of some uninterrupted time. Begin by reread-

ing your answers to EXERCISE 1. This will help you access your feelings.

FIRST: Review all the words on the FEELINGS LIST. Identify any words that describe your feelings during or immediately after your miscarriage and write them on a separate piece of paper to include in your GRN. (The list below is not intended to be all-inclusive. Feel free to use other words not found on the FEELINGS LIST that nevertheless accurately portray your emotions.)

❖ FEELINGS LIST ❖

depressed	angry	discouraged
despondent	helpless	bitter
fatigued	hopeless	pessimistic
punished	tense	short-tempered
grouchy	nervous	sarcastic
weary	tearful	irritable
annoyed	enraged	sad
distraught	lonely	isolated
despairing	shattered	alone
guilty	relieved	fearful
jealous	responsible	anxious
unfulfilled	joyless	confused

SECOND: Now it is time to put your own personal meaning to the words you have selected. This process will help you better understand why you feel what you feel. On a separate piece of paper use each word you have chosen in a feeling sentence to describe your emotion and include your sentences in your GRN.

For example:

> Feeling: *Anger*
> Sentence: *I felt anger at God because He let*
>   *my baby die.*

EXERCISE 6: *Expressing Your Feelings*

After you identify your feelings using EXERCISE 5, spend some time expressing them. Why is this necessary? When you express your feelings you begin to release your emotional pain and this brings you another step closer to experiencing true healing.

Your particular means of expression probably will vary according to your gifts and preferences. That's great, just trust your instincts. I love to write; consequently my most cathartic work is done when I put written words to my feelings. However, anything that seems to "fit" for you is a good choice. Consider some of the following options:

❖ journaling

❖ sharing with a safe person

❖ praying

❖ writing a letter to God

❖ painting

❖ drawing

❖ writing song lyrics

❖ composing music

❖ sculpting

❖ writing poetry or a fictional story using your feelings as a motivating theme.

Your work can be included in your **GRN**. Additionally, you may choose to include some of your work in your baby's scrapbook (see **CHAPTER TWELVE**).

Chapter Four

FOR HUSBANDS AND WIVES

"The goal in marriage is not to think alike,
but to think together."

— *Robert C. Dodds*

I never saw Laird cry over the death of our first baby. He always listened attentively to me, speaking to me in that very soft, soothing way he has. He held me as I sobbed, tenderly stroked my hair, and promised me that things would get better. But I never saw him **grieve** the death of our first child. I watched him sit in front of the television for hours, seemingly mesmerized by the silliest shows, while I secretly seethed. "How can he watch television when our baby has just died? He seems so unaffected by this whole nightmare!" Only later did I realize that Laird was using television to help him escape his grief. Perhaps I never realized the extent of Laird's pain because I expected him to grieve the same way I did. I was looking for tears, for him to evidence some need to talk about the miscarriage and his feelings. Why? Because that was how I dealt with my pain. In my

51

quest to get Laird to conform to my style of grief expression, I missed his pain and the opportunity for us to grieve together.

Sometimes tragedies bring people closer together. Other times, however, they can push people further apart. Sadly, miscarriages often divide husbands and wives, partially because of the differences in the way men and women handle their grief. It is not uncommon for a female miscarriage survivor to experience and express her emotions with an intensity that overwhelms her husband. He may be frightened by her seeming lack of control, uncomfortable with her style of expression, unsure how to respond to her, or so distressed by his wife's pain that he ignores his own feelings while trying desperately to alleviate her agony.

While women may be openly expressive, men are typically less verbal and self-revealing about their grief feelings. A man may reserve his tears for private, exhibiting very little observable pain in public. Because of this, a wife may incorrectly assume that her husband does not care about their miscarriage. What can result is a growing chasm between husband and wife resulting from a lack of communication and supportive sharing. This was the case when Michael and Jennifer sought counseling because their relationship had become increasingly strained after their second miscarriage. Tearfully, Jennifer expressed both her growing resentment and her confusion regarding her husband's reactions to their losses.

> *I can't understand why Michael doesn't care about the loss of our babies. He just goes right on with his life like nothing ever happened. He says he's hurting, but he never shows it. I'm starting to think that maybe Michael doesn't even want children.*

Michael then shared his side of the story.

I do want to have children and I am sad about our babies. Jennifer doesn't understand my grief because I don't show my feelings the same way she does. She seems to be crying and depressed all the time. In the beginning, I was sympathetic and supportive of her. But now, well... I'm just getting a little bit tired of her tears. She always seems to want to talk about the miscarriages and I just don't have anything left to say.

This kind of marital tension is quite common after a couple has suffered a miscarriage. If these problems are not confronted and resolved, the marriage will suffer. Michael and Jennifer recognized the conflicts in their relationship and they chose to get professional help. We worked on several different concerns in their marriage, focusing on their communication skills. They both learned to put words to their own feelings and to listen empathically while their partner shared. Eventually, they were able to accept each other's way of handling painful emotions and to appreciate the differences in their styles. Michael learned how to support Jennifer without feeling the need to fix her pain. Because of this, he felt more freedom to express his own hurts and needs. Jennifer stopped pressuring Michael to talk and found herself listening more carefully to what he was willing to share about his feelings. She actually discovered that he had a lot to say!

Michael and Jennifer are excellent examples of what can be accomplished in a hurting marriage when both partners are committed to each other and to making changes for the health of their relationship. Possibly you, too, are feeling overwhelmed by your pain and very distant from your partner. Don't give up! You and your spouse can survive this difficult time if you choose to work together and support each other. Effective communication is a critical part of this healing process because it allows partners the opportunity to share their deepest feelings and to be understood by someone they love.

LISTENING SKILLS

Very few couples will argue with the fact that their communication skills could use some fine tuning. Most people, however, feel lost as to where and how to begin to make positive changes. One of the best starting points is to learn how to practice the following two types of active listening techniques: 1) empathic listening and 2) reflective listening.

Empathic listening differs from the everyday listening that you and I use most of the time. Listening empathically involves very little, if any, verbal feedback from the listener. As the listener, you will listen carefully to everything your spouse says without getting distracted, impatient, critical, or judgmental. Make sure you maintain good eye contact with the speaker (your spouse) and that you use your facial expressions to communicate understanding. A gentle touch (for example: a hug, or light touch on the arm) can also effectively communicate support to your spouse. If you cannot understand or do not share your spouse's feelings, DO NOT pass judgment with your words or your body language (a frown, a raised eyebrow, etc.). If you do not understand and you want clarification, wait until your spouse has finished sharing and ask for clarification in a respectful manner (choose your words and tone of voice carefully).

Reflective listening incorporates all the skills you practice in empathic listening and then builds upon them.

When you listen to the speaker, you listen intently so that you are able to summarize verbally both his emotions and his content when he is finished speaking. Basically you will be *reflecting* or mirroring what your spouse has just said. When first learning this skill, some couples feel awkward and silly. I often hear a spouse respond, "I heard her. I know what she said." It is important that you verbally reflect back what your spouse has said even if you are convinced you heard and understood everything completely. (You would be surprised how often I witness a spouse incorrectly reflecting a partner's feelings and needs!) This then gives your spouse the opportunity to correct or clarify any misunderstandings and to elaborate on a point that may be confusing. When couples do not practice this technique, miscommunications can grow and fester, often without the knowledge of either partner.

In the beginning, it may be difficult to appreciate the tangible advantages of learning and practicing these particular communication skills. Rehearsing a new skill until it becomes a habit can feel quite unnatural. However, if you read the following examples of ineffective and effective communication, I believe you will notice some crucial differences immediately. Additionally, as you review the analysis of these examples, I think you will understand how critical empathic listening and reflective listening skills can be in creating a solid communication foundation.

COUPLE #1

Wife (speaker): "I feel very sad most of the time. Sometimes I just want to be held and comforted. Then other times, I want to climb in bed and hide from the world. You know, everybody get away and leave me alone!"

Husband (listener): "You just want me to leave you alone."

COUPLE #2

Wife (speaker): "I feel very sad most of the time. Sometimes I just want to be held and comforted. Then other times, I want to climb in bed and hide from the world. You know, everybody get away and leave me alone!"

Husband (listener): "You have mixed needs. Sometimes when you feel sad you want comfort and sometimes you want privacy."

In this example it is easy to see that the response of the husband in the second couple is much more accurate and, therefore, more effective than the response of the husband in the first couple. The effective response enhances the communication process because it conveys the message, "I'm listening carefully and trying hard to understand how you feel." When partners feel empathy and a willingness to understand originating from each other, communication opens up and has the potential to deepen. Often new levels of vulnerability and emotional intimacy are reached.

However, when an ineffective response similar to the one in the Couple #1 example is received, the speaker may shut down. You see, whether intentionally or unintentionally, the listener has just sent the underlying message, "I'm not really listening. Let's get through this as quickly as possible." Although a partner receiving this type of message will probably be frustrated and perhaps angry, the communication process is not hopeless *because this couple is verbalizing their conclusions and assumptions by practicing reflective listening skills*. This fact gives the speaker an opportunity to correct the listener's inaccurate conclusions by providing clarification or specific examples until the husband can accurately summarize the wife's feelings and needs. Imagine what would happen if this couple simply bypassed the reflective listening process! The husband would silently draw his erroneous conclusions and adjust his behavior accordingly. He may distance himself from his wife, truly believing that privacy is the only thing she wants and that he is being a good husband by leaving her alone. The wife, whose needs are more complex than her husband assumes, may then begin to feel alienated from and abandoned by her husband when she needs him most. She may then begin to form her own conclusions (probably inaccurate) about her husband's feelings based on his actions and alter her behavior accordingly. Do you see how this omission — the choice to remain silent rather than to verbalize and to check their assumptions — has triggered a miscommunication avalanche plunging downhill? I have seen couples in my office that have allowed this process to go unchecked for years. Believe me, these avalanches can become incredibly destructive.

Your communication does not have to deteriorate into a negative pattern threatening to destroy your relationship. You can choose to use your miscarriage experience as an opportunity to improve your communication and enhance your intimacy level. The raw painfulness of your tragedy may allow you to discover previously unacknowledged feelings. This deeper awareness of your emotions then gives you the opportunity to express them, understand them, and grow together from your experience. The following exercises will enable each of you to access both your feelings and your needs at this point in your grieving process and to practice constructive listening skills.

EXERCISE 7: Enhancing Communication

(This exercise works better if both partners have already completed the exercises in Chapter Three.)

FIRST: You and your spouse write **separate** feeling statements describing your current feelings. This is similar to EXERCISE 5 except you are limiting your sentences to your **present** emotional state. Sometimes a partner will believe that he is finished with his feelings about the miscarriage and has nothing new to bring to this exercise. If this is the case for you, use this exercise to help you understand your spouse's present feelings. Explore any feelings you may have in response to your spouse's current emotions and needs reflected in these next exercises.

For example:

I feel *guilty* because *I think the miscarriage is my fault.*

SECOND: Now both of you will elaborate on your feelings by adding a need statement to the end of your feeling statement. This sentence is intended to be a specific request you make of your spouse regarding your needs. As a result of this exercise, your partner should be aware of your tangible need and therefore more likely to respond to your need.

For example:

I feel guilty because I think the miscarriage is my fault, and I need you to reassure me that I'm not to blame.

EXERCISE 8: Listening Reflectively

Secure a quiet place where you and your spouse can share your feeling and need statements without interruption. Listen intently to one another's feelings and needs **without judgment**. Practice your new reflective listening skills by verbally summarizing what you heard your spouse say after he or she is finished talking. (Remember to include the principles of empathic listening, too.)

EXERCISE 9: *Praying Together*

Connie and Tim's premature son was stillborn and their sorrow was profound. Despite this, they chose to cling to each other and to God during their grief. Eventually, they found that some of their most healing moments came when they held hands and prayed together, asking for God's grace and mercy. Tim's sincerity was evident as he told me about the difference prayer had made in their grieving process.

> *We didn't even know where to start or really how to talk to God about this. But we just started to let our feelings out and just kind of talked to Him about everything. We cried a lot and we even got angry a few times. It seemed to really help us to pray together because then we knew more about what the other person was thinking...*

I believe that sometimes God allows us to endure grief in order to bring us closer to Him. Often we get so busy with our lives that we don't spend time nurturing our relationship with God. Have you noticed how time seems to stand still when you're grieving? Suddenly all those very important things in life don't seem so crucial and you may feel the need for God's presence more keenly than ever. Perhaps God is calling you to seek Him — to renew your relationship with Him.

You and your spouse also can use your common faith in God to help you grow closer together in this time of sorrow, just as Connie and Tim did. Spend some time in prayer together. Talk to God about your pain, your feelings, and your needs. Pray even if you can only bring your anger to God at this time. He is big enough to handle anything you bring to Him.

SEX AND GRIEF

When they came into my office, Jodie and Paul had been sniping at each other for weeks since Jodie's second-trimester miscarriage. Jodie fired off the first verbal shot.

> *I'm so tired I just want to be left alone so I can get some sleep. Paul just doesn't get it. He constantly pressures me for sex.*

Paul shot right back at her.

> *Well, I'm tired too. I'm tired of being put off. I'm tired of waiting for you to feel "in the mood." When are things going to be normal again?*

Just as a miscarriage can break down marital communication, it can also shatter your sexual relationship. As we explored Jodie and Paul's feelings, we discovered that Jodie shared the concerns and emotions that many women confront after a miscarriage. It is not unusual for women to be reluctant to resume sex after losing their baby for fear of getting pregnant and suffering another miscarriage. Sometimes post-miscarriage depression and fatigue are so overwhelming that sexual desire is virtually nonexistent. During this post-miscarriage phase, a woman's hormones are undergoing a readjustment as they return to pre-pregnancy levels and this can affect sexual desire and energy. (This hormonal readjustment process takes an average of six weeks, depending on the circumstances of the loss. Talk with your medical doctor to get an idea of what you can expect as you **physically** recover from your miscarriage.)

Your husband may be feeling a similar disinterest in sex or he may be exasperated by your lack of interest just as Paul was annoyed with Jodie. Although frustrating and painful, this disruption in your sex life is a common response to miscarriage. Most likely it will pass as long as you practice patience, understanding, and clear communication with one another. Jodie and Paul found this to be true for them. Once they understood the emotional and physical reasons behind Jodie's "hands off" policy, they shifted their focus from sex to intimacy. They found through practicing effective communication skills that there were non-sexual ways of experiencing intimacy which, in turn, helped them feel close and connected emotionally. Because she now had Paul's emotional support, Jodie was able to gain trust in him and to triumph over her fears about resuming sex. Their sexual relationship actually benefited from their more vulnerable communication!

An equally common sexual response to miscarriage is what I call the **_Let's Have Another Baby Right Away Syndrome_**. Tammy and Philip, members of my support group, were struggling with this issue. One evening, Tammy shared her thoughts with the other members.

> _I just want to try again right away. Is that bad? I can hardly wait until the doctor gives us the okay. I feel like we are just losing valuable time._

After a miscarriage, many couples feel a compelling urge to try to get pregnant again immediately. It is a common experience among miscarriage survivors to try to fill their void with another pregnancy as soon as possible. Husbands and wives need to approach the idea of trying to conceive again with caution. Make sure that the two of you are in **agreement** about the timing and that you both have worked through your grief to the point that you feel emotionally ready to try again. I have talked to many couples in these circumstances wherein one partner assumed that the other partner was ready to try to conceive again when, in reality, the partner was not ready. This conflict regarding such a life altering decision inevitably leads to other problems and misunderstandings. (That reflective listening can come in handy!)

As you consider the question of when to try to conceive again, keep in mind your obstetrician's recommendation about resuming intercourse. Most doctors will recommend waiting between two to six weeks (depending on various medical factors) before resuming intercourse and between two to three normal menstrual cycles before trying to get pregnant again. It is critical for a woman to feel physically (as well as emotionally) ready to handle another pregnancy, particularly if the last pregnancy created or exacerbated health concerns. Any questions about your physical health and another pregnancy should be addressed with your physician.

EXERCISE 10: Understanding your Feelings about Sex

This exercise is intended to help you and your spouse clarify and communicate your present feelings about sex and about trying to conceive another child. Since your feelings about resuming sex can be complicated and perhaps even ambivalent, it is important for you to accurately determine what you are feeling so that you can then help your spouse understand your needs.

FIRST: On a separate piece of paper, list your feelings about resuming sex.

For example:

I feel fearful about having sex because I'm afraid of having another miscarriage.

SECOND: If sex does not feel emotionally safe right now, list some other ways you and your spouse can demonstrate love and support for one another. (Include both part I and II in your GRN.)

For example:

We can snuggle together in front of the fireplace.

THIRD: You and your spouse should find a quiet place and share your lists with one another. Keep in mind you are both grieving and your goal should be to find ways to mutually support and nurture one another. It is not necessary to have the same feelings and needs about sex. (In fact, it is likely that you will not.) Search for ways to compromise. If you accomplish this, your sex life will resume naturally as an extension of the intimacy you and your spouse have worked hard to create. (Be sure to practice your new listening skills!)

Chapter Five

THE QUEST FOR "WHY?"

*"There are many theological questions which
can be asked — even interesting ones,
for which the truest answer this side
of the grave is, 'I don't know.'"*

—James A. Pike

orking in the area of grief recovery has provided me with the opportunity to help many people — and for that I feel truly blessed. My work has also brought me face to face with countless tragic stories and wounded people searching to find meaning in the midst of their pain. Lorrie wrote me the following letter sharing her desperate need to understand why she continued to suffer agonizing losses.

*I just don't get it. After a while I could
make sense of my first miscarriage. I mean,
the timing was wrong for a baby. Greg was
still in school and we were living with his
parents. Even the second miscarriage*

taught me some things about my priorities.
I began putting God first, I joined a be-
reaved parents' support group, and I even
got more involved in the leadership of the
support group so I could use my pain in a
positive way... to help others. But after our
third miscarriage and a stillborn son, I want
to know WHY?! Why would God keep al-
lowing this to happen? Is there some lesson
we're missing?

Lorrie is definitely not alone. WHY? seems to be the question haunting the majority of miscarriage survivors. Even when people differ about the way their grief manifests itself, I have yet to meet a miscarriage survivor who did not ask WHY? at some point. It is human nature to try to make sense of your pain — to try to find some meaning in the midst of your tragedy. Many Christians believe that God teaches His children through their trials, so they look for a spiritual lesson to help ease the pain of miscarriage. You, too, may believe that if you can find a spiritual purpose in your loss, God will not need to allow another miscarriage because you have learned your lesson. Others of you may look for medical reasons for your miscarriage. In either of these cases, the situation may then seem medically fixable or spiritually understandable and this yields a feeling of control. This sense of control, in turn, instills hope in grieving parents.

But what happens when miscarriage survivors cannot find the answers to WHY? What if there seem to be no readily apparent lessons from God, and the doctors have no medical explanations? Grieving parents in this circumstance can feel that preventing another loss is totally outside their own control. The resulting feelings of helplessness can sometimes translate into hopelessness and despair.

It is natural human reaction to search for reasons for your suffering to help you cope. Often when people search for meaning to their pain, they are able to see some constructive growth result from their loss. However, God will not always reveal *His* plan in *your* timing. Additionally, there may be no obvious medical problem to remedy in your case. Frequently, grieving parents must face the reality that no answers are forthcoming from God, their doctors, or the medical community at large. Sometimes the only answer you will hear is, "We don't know for sure. This is a random biological occurrence."

Many miscarriage survivors have told me that, with time, they were able to make sense of their first loss. However, they struggled intensely with the purpose for subsequent losses. One lady told me, "I naively thought I had paid my dues. I felt confident that I would not lose another baby. Boy, was I wrong." I must admit that I, too, believed I had "paid my dues" after my first miscarriage.

Laird and I lost our first child in a first-trimester miscarriage and our doctor explained that my pregnancy was probably never viable — which apparently meant it was doomed from the point of conception. This bit of medical semantics meant very little to me because I believed I was carrying a baby, not simply a blighted ovum. Our baby's death was devastating and I often felt very alone. However, as a result of my suffering and my personal healing process, this book, the Empty Arms support group and ministry (for parents who have suffered a miscarriage, stillbirth, or infant death), and my grief recovery workshops were created. In time, I was able to see a purpose for my loss because God was using my experience in a positive way to reach other hurting parents.

When I got pregnant for the second time, I began cramping almost immediately after the doctor confirmed the results of my positive home pregnancy test. When I first discovered that I was also spotting, I panicked. "Oh, dear God. Please, no!" A detached resignation rapidly followed this initial fear. "Oh well, it's happening again. At least this time I know what to expect." I remember being in a perpetual state of readiness to experience another miscarriage. Thankfully, my physical and emotional condition improved around the fifth month of pregnancy and Laird and I felt great joy at the miraculous birth of our healthy son, Jordan, four months later.

When I became pregnant the third time, I felt more confident that God would allow our baby to come to full term since I had been able to carry and deliver Jordan successfully. In fact, after his birth I felt oddly reassured that we had already endured our token miscarriage, learned our lessons, and we were now ready for smooth pregnancies and healthy deliveries. Blissfully ignorant and steeped in my faulty thinking, I never imagined what the next few weeks would bring us.

A FALLEN LEAF

"Well, that little one must be moving all around. I just can't seem to find a heartbeat."

I was fifteen weeks pregnant and the nurse practitioner could not find the baby's heartbeat. The nurse did an excellent job hiding her alarm as she said to me cheerfully with a smiling face, "But don't worry — it's not unusual at this age since the baby has a lot of space to move around in. Sometimes these little ones just like to go exploring. Why don't we give the doctor a go at it?"

The doctor was also unable to find the baby's heartbeat and she suggested we schedule an ultrasound for the next day as a routine precautionary measure. Remarkably, I still felt no real concern or anxiety. After all, I was still throwing up everything I ate or drank which is supposed to mean that the fetus is developing normally and causing hormonal changes to which my body was reacting. Also, the doctor had just heard a strong heart-beat two days before. Besides, God wouldn't let me progress this far into a pregnancy only to lose the baby — I felt certain of that. So I left the doctor's office excited about the prospect of seeing our little baby on the screen during my unexpected ultrasound.

Laird was able to get some time off work to accom-pany me to the ultrasound. Once again, I bloated myself with the suggested 32 ounces of water and we headed to-wards the doctor's office, chatting about baby names and wondering if we would be able to tell the gender of our baby from the sonogram. As I lay on the table, I saw our baby's form come into view on the monitor. Instantly I knew something was wrong. "There's no heartbeat. I don't see a heartbeat," I whispered in horror, grabbing Laird's hand. Laird squinted at the screen and then turned expectantly toward the technician, waiting for her reassurance that everything was fine. I knew better. Any-one who has seen his or her living baby in utero on a sonogram screen knows that the heartbeat is visibly noticeable and that the baby is typically bouncing, float-ing, or moving in some way. Our baby was completely motionless. Laird and I were stunned.

The technician looked at me awkwardly and said, "Are you okay? I need to go across the hall and talk to the doctor to see what she wants to do now."

I nodded numbly and she left us alone with the image of our lifeless baby seared into our minds. Laird helped me off the table and I fumbled to get dressed. All I could think of was how much I wanted to get out of that room.

The car ride home was eerily quiet; both of us staring out the window. Mindlessly, I fidgeted with my wedding ring and tried to clean the spots off my sunglasses, won-dering why I couldn't seem to cry. Once we were home, however, we sobbed and held each other for a very long time. Later that day we rallied our friends and family around us, asking them to pray for a healing miracle. We had heard wonderful stories of babies who had appeared dead in ultrasound pictures and then miraculously lived! Nothing is too great for our God! I poured my energy into the hope that God would use our situation to work a miracle that would touch the lives of people around us. There was to be no miracle this time, however. Sadly, our baby's heart remained silent and still.

Our next step was to review our options with our doctor. She explained to us that because of our baby's physical size, I could not have a simple D & C. I was going to have to go to the hospital and be induced for labor. "It's usually a long process. Labor in these kinds of cases lasts about twelve hours," she warned us. Then she called the hospital to make the arrangements.

After a sleepless night, Laird and I arrived at the hospital admissions office at 6:30 a.m. "I'm here for a fetal demise induction," I informed the clerk, quoting the terminology my doctor had instructed me to use. The clerk stopped making small talk and completed my paperwork with remarkable haste.

When we reached my room on the maternity ward, I noticed a picture of a fallen leaf on a dew-covered ground was taped to the door. Later I discovered this was the hospital code for "Fetal Demise In Progress. Please Do Not Put a Pregnant Woman in Labor in This Room!" Although this leaf picture felt a bit like a scarlet letter, I was thankful that I did not have to worry about having a hospital roommate during this experience.

The next step was to get hooked up to my I.V. and have my blood drawn. Because I was dehydrated and thirteen pounds under weight as a result of being sick from my pregnancy, both of these procedures turned out to be miserable ordeals. My veins kept collapsing or rolling and the nurse was forced to stick me over and over again with her needles. Eventually, she succeeded and then the official induction process began. Every two hours the nurse administered labor-inducing medication and recorded all my vital signs. Fortunately, my first nurse was a gentle, soft-spoken woman who pampered me shamelessly, bringing me pre-warmed blankets, patting my forehead with a cool washcloth, and calling me "honey" and "sweetie."

The hours drudged by with interminable monotony. Laird and my sister Tracey (she had come to offer comfort and company) read magazines, watched television, asked me how I was doing, and ate. Breakfast...Lunch...Dinner. Not being permitted to drink or eat anything other than ice chips, I first eyed their cheeseburgers with envy. Then, however, the medication to induce labor caused nausea and my hunger was completely forgotten. Soon my back and shoulders ached from retching, my head felt like it was going to explode from searing pain, my contractions gradually intensified, and I lost a sea of blood.

My second nurse was a woman who seemed more interested in watching the television in my room than in performing her duties with compassion or gentleness. She rarely spoke to me or announced her presence. The first indication I got that she was in the room was when she would roll me over like a sack of potatoes and slap a blood pressure cuff on my arm. And every two hours, she revisited my room to torture me all over again.

I saw my doctor only a few times during this seemingly endless nightmare. "Why is this taking so long?" I asked. "You said twelve hours." She always reassured me that it would be "soon, very soon."

Twenty-one hours after labor induction began, I delivered our baby daughter, Diandra. "I've ordered a genetics workup on this baby," the doctor instructed the nurse. I was relieved that she was going to try to find out a reason for our baby's death. "Well," replied the nurse as she turned our baby over on her back, "you don't need the whole thing. I can just cut a piece out of its back."

I was absolutely speechless! Was this nurse really standing inches away from me referring to my baby as a "thing" and talking about cutting a chunk out of her back? Surely, I must be hallucinating from lack of food, water, and sleep! But no, that was my last distinct memory of the short time we had with Diandra. Quickly, an orderly shuffled me off to an operating room for a D & C so the doctor could recover the placenta which had not delivered on its own.

Unfortunately, the results from the genetics testing on Diandra yielded very little information. During the aftermath of this wretched experience, I remember feeling outrage at what I perceived as God's deliberate disregard for me, my needs, and my prayers. I felt incredibly insignificant to God at that time. After all, hadn't I fervently and faithfully prayed that God would only allow me to become pregnant if I could carry the baby to full term and deliver her safely? Then, once I had become pregnant hadn't I continued to pray for the baby's healthy development? I thought I had covered all the bases with my prayers. But my logic was human and, while it made perfect sense to me, it was not God's plan.

Many people have asked me how I came to a place of acceptance even without a sense of purpose for my daughter's death. First, it was not an immediate acceptance. I agonized over WHY? Frankly, even today I have no answer to the question of why my daughter had to die. All I know is that God allowed her death for His own purpose, and I may not know that purpose until I meet Him (and my daughter) in heaven. Perhaps the best answer I can give is that I remained open to accepting God's comfort and mercy in the various forms that He sent them to me. I also **chose** to let go of my need to know why Diandra died. I knew from my professional and personal experiences that I had to confront and deal with my grief, so I did many of the things recommended in this book. (Yes, I really try to practice what I preach!) I also prayed consistently for God's peace and comfort. Mercifully, He sent people to support me and to listen to me. Gently, He reminded me of the many blessings in my life — a wonderful husband, a beautiful son, supportive friends and family (just to name a few). And eventually, He blessed me with another miraculous gift — the birth of our second son, Carson, fifteen months after Diandra's death.

Often people ask if I would be at peace not having my two boys — if I were childless. Honestly, I do not know the answer to that question. I do know that God would be there for me. But I would have to make the choice to come to Him. No doubt it would be incredibly difficult for me to work through the grief of being unable to bear a child just as it is for many people who experience childlessness. However, I have also seen people unable to bear their own children who go on to give their love to others in a variety of wonderful and fulfilling ways.

Finding a place of peace and acceptance concerning your baby's death will be a challenge. As my own story illustrates, healing is a process that takes time and involves trying to make sense of your loss — asking WHY? Perhaps you are grappling with similar questions of WHY? and having a hard time letting go of your dream of "what could have been." What a challenge it is to accept God's timing when it so harshly conflicts with your own plans. The following exercises are designed to help you find peace as you struggle to accept God's timing and search for your own answers.

EXERCISE 11: *Asking Questions*

I do believe that God can and does use our life experiences to teach us. Sometimes the purpose of a tragedy is discernible and we can learn and grow from our pain. Use your natural inclination to ask WHY? to determine the answers to the following questions:

1. ASK GOD

❖ What are You teaching my spouse and me?

❖ Pray that He will reveal His purpose to you and that in the meantime He will comfort you, encourage you, direct you, and give you patience and hope.

❖ List any answers you receive from God.

2. ASK YOUR DOCTOR

❖ Do my spouse and/or I have any medical conditions that may predispose us to miscarriage?

❖ If the answer is yes, have the doctor give you a thorough explanation and supply you with options.

❖ If a genetics work-up was ordered after your miscarriage, have the results explained thoroughly — again reviewing your options.

EXERCISE 12: *Accepting Unanswered Questions*

There will also be times when you do not understand the reason for your pain and answers do not seem forthcoming. Once you have asked the obvious and important questions, your most challenging task awaits. Now it is time to accept the answers you have and to *accept the answers you do not have.*

1. Write down each of your unanswered questions on a separate piece of paper. Light a fire in your fireplace (or some other appropriate and safe place) and, together with your spouse, place each question, one at a time, in the flames. This is your way of symbolically letting go of your need to know WHY?

2. Pray together that God will take these questions and your need to have answers and that He will carry this burden for you. Ask Him to release you from your desire to know WHY?, to fill you with His peace, and to give you hope for the future.

Chapter Six

NOT GUILTY!

*"There is little room left for wisdom
when one is full of judgment."*

— Malcolm Hein

lthough guilt was not a troubling issue for me with my first miscarriage, I did experience guilt after my second loss. During my second, third, and fourth pregnancies I was diagnosed with a medical condition known as hyperemesis. Basically, this means I was so severely ill with nausea and vomiting that I lost a lot of weight and became dehydrated. In fact, it is not unusual for a pregnant mother with this condition to end up in the hospital hooked up to an I.V. Needless to say, this is a miserable condition which afflicts a small percentage of pregnant women and requires close medical attention to ensure the health of the mother and fetus.

Shortly before my daughter's heart stopped in utero, my doctor wanted to hospitalize me because I had lost thirteen pounds, was becoming dangerously dehydrated, and I was unable to keep fluids down at home. Since I had an eighteen month-old son at home who needed me, I begged her to give me a chance to rehydrate myself at home. Because my baby's heartbeat was strong and I

promised to follow her strict instructions, she agreed as
long as I came back to see her in two days. I followed her
instructions religiously and was able to get myself out of
the danger zone. Despite my effort, our baby still died. I
couldn't shake the nagging thought that it had been my
lack of adequate fluid intake that had killed our baby.

My doctor assured me that she did not believe the two
things were connected. "The majority of women who
suffer hyperemesis give birth to healthy babies. You had
hyperemesis with Jordan and he was a big, healthy baby."

I also had hyperemesis during my fourth pregnancy
with Carson, and he was also a big, healthy baby at birth.
Still I had to grapple with the lingering doubt and feelings of responsibility.

As the previous chapter discussed, miscarriage survivors often look for reasons for their losses. Sometimes
this pursuit for reasons can even become a process of placing blame on someone (the doctor, the hospital, the stress
of the workplace, God). Sadly, all too often women blame
themselves just as I had done. The following comments
are fears of guilt and responsibility that I hear frequently
from women who have just lost a baby:

> *My mother never had a miscarriage. I
> have two sisters and they've never had any
> miscarriages. I feel like I must have done
> something wrong. I just can't figure out
> what....*

> *I was taking a medication that my
> doctor said was okay, but I'm not so sure
> now.*

> *My doctor said it was all right for me
> to continue my aerobics, but what if that's
> what caused my miscarriage?*

I'm certain that I lost my baby because I drank a couple glasses of wine over the Christmas holidays before I knew I was pregnant.

My pregnancy was unexpected and, well, I wasn't very excited about it in the beginning. It wasn't a good time in my life to have a baby. I was just starting to get excited about having a baby and then... I think God was punishing me for my bad attitude.

I had bad eating habits. I should have eaten more healthy foods.

I was under a tremendous amount of stress at work.

My husband and I were arguing a lot back then. We were even talking about divorce.

I was having bad headaches before I knew I was pregnant and I was taking aspirin all the time.

These are some of the most common guilt statements I hear. In fact, you may be blaming yourself right now using one of these reasons or another reason of your own. Perhaps even your spouse, your family, or your friends are also blaming you. You may feel their judgment through their probing questions or their silent stares. If you feel responsible for your miscarriage, you are carrying a lot of guilt and you are not alone. However, in the vast majority of cases, **the miscarriage is not the mother's fault.** Carrying around the weight of feeling responsible for your baby's death is a tremendous and often unnecessary burden.

First, in order to free yourself from the burden of guilt, you must begin to educate yourself on the reasons for miscarriage. (You may have already done this in your quest for WHY? from the preceding chapter.) You can read books, magazines, and pamphlets. You can talk with your doctor. As you continue this process of education, you will most likely find that your miscarriage was not your fault. If however, you find that you did put yourself at risk by smoking, drinking alcohol, using illegal drugs or prescription drugs unsafe for a fetus, you can choose to take care of your body so that you can put your mind at ease for future pregnancies and can avoid the guilt trap. If guilt continues to haunt you, professional counseling may be a good option for you at this point in your grief recovery process.

EXERCISE 13: Healthy Preparation

Although you did not cause your miscarriage, it is always in the best interest of both you and your baby to take care of yourself during the time you are trying to conceive and after you become pregnant. (In fact, healthy living is the preferred choice in any circumstance!) The following list contains widely accepted recommendations for women who are pregnant or trying to become pregnant. If you have any concerns about items on this list, do not hesitate to discuss them with your medical doctor.

- ❖ Abstain from alcoholic beverages.

- ❖ Abstain from smoking.
  NOTE: Even **second-hand** smoke has been proven to be a health hazard.

- ❖ Check with your doctor or pharmacist before using any prescription medication.

❖ Do NOT use illegal drugs.

❖ Take a prenatal vitamin or a multivitamin with the recommended dosage of folic acid for women of child-bearing years. Check with your doctor or pharmacist regarding this.

❖ Get early prenatal care. Discuss your miscarriage history with your doctor.

❖ If you have any doubts about whether or not to exercise, discuss your concerns with your doctor.

❖ Avoid consuming caffeine and aspartame (i.e.: Nutrasweet).

❖ Eat a healthy diet. Your doctor can recommend one.

❖ Get plenty of rest and drink plenty of water.

EXERCISE 14: A Not Guilty Verdict

Have you ever noticed that if you tell yourself something repeatedly, you begin to believe it's true? Some of the women I see for grief counseling are sending themselves continuous GUILTY messages and they have begun to believe these messages are true. This exercise is designed to help remind you in a very tangible way that you are not guilty for your baby's death.

Take a blank 3 x 5 card and write in large bold letters the words NOT GUILTY on it. Post this card in a conspicuous place so that you will see it on a daily basis (your bathroom mirror, your refrigerator, your car dashboard, etc.). Each time you look at it say aloud, "I am not guilty for my miscarriage." Continue to do this until you truly believe that you are not guilty.

Chapter Seven

HANDLING
YOUR ANGER

"Anger conquers when unresolved."

— Anonymous

or as long as I can remember, I have had a keen sense of fair play, despite the fact that I know that life is not fair. Typically, I strive to live my life by a set of fairness standards and I have definite opinions about what is fair and how to accomplish fairness in life. (Needless to say, this trait is NOT on my husband's list of the Top Ten Reasons Why I Love My Wife.) In the past I operated from the premise that since I want what is fair and God is fair, God will do what I want. As you can imagine, this faulty logic has caused me to feel disillusioned and disappointed on numerous occasions. Thankfully, with God's help I have begun to examine the apparent inequities in my life with a different perspective.

Nonetheless, when I suffered my miscarriages, my sense of fair play went haywire. Absolutely nothing about my losses seemed fair to me and I was quick to entertain self-pitying thoughts. During the aftermath of my first miscarriage, I had an acute attack of the "It's Not Fairs" that went something like this:

> *It's not fair that it took us so long to conceive only to lose our baby.*
>
> *It's not fair that so many undeserving parents have no difficulty conceiving a child or carrying one to full term.* (At the time, there was a local news story of a couple living out of their car who allowed their pet rat to maul their six month-old baby to death. This kind of story is difficult for most of us to fathom, but it seemed particularly tragic and senseless to me during my time of grief.)
>
> *It's not fair to lose a baby for whom so many prayers were said.*

Although the circumstances were different, I also felt a sense of injustice after our second loss. In December 1992, I dragged myself into my doctor's office for a number of physical complaints — bad headaches, fatigue, insomnia, to name a few. (I usually have to have a litany of symptoms before I am willing to make a doctor's appointment!) While I was in the examining room, I embarrassedly asked the doctor if he could remove a small, ugly mole from my upper right thigh. I felt quite self-conscious about making the request — it seemed a little vain to me. Fortunately, the doctor's patient load was light that day and he was able to remove the mole immediately so I was spared another trip to the doctor. As I was leaving, my physician informed me that he would send the mole into the lab for a routine biopsy and that I could expect his office to phone me with the results in two weeks.

Despite the fact that I had no reason to be concerned, I began phoning the doctor's office daily once the biopsy results were past due. (I hate loose ends!) Finally, the nurse realized she couldn't stall anymore and she put the doctor on the phone to speak to me.

"I have your biopsy results and they are not good. You have a malignant melanoma. Do you know what that is?" I did not. "This is cancer and it is a very somber diagnosis. I want you in my office tomorrow morning at 7:00 a.m. so that we can begin to run tests." He then asked me if I was going to be okay and if he could speak to Laird.

After Laird finished discussing my condition with the doctor, he came downstairs to find me sitting, cold, pale, and motionless in our darkened living room.

I soon learned that malignant melanoma is an aggressive and potentially deadly form of skin cancer. I had always been very healthy, but this diagnosis forced me to confront my own mortality. During the next few weeks when my prognosis was uncertain, there were moments when I despaired, "I'm going to die and my own son won't even remember me. He won't remember what it felt like to be rocked to sleep by his mommy. He won't remember my laugh, my smile, my voice. It will be as if I never existed in his life!" Fortunately, God was faithful as always, helping me cope with my fears and nightmares. One dark and rainy day I was consumed by the futility of trying to fight CANCER, when I heard what I believed to be God's voice in my mind. "Shari, I am greater than any cancer." For me, that moment was both a source of great comfort and a convicting reminder of His omnipotence.

Not only do I believe that God spoke to me on that bleak day, but I also believe the physical symptoms that prompted me to make that initial doctor's appointment were a God-given smoke screen to get me prompt healthcare for my melanoma. Mysteriously, all those symptoms for which I made the initial doctor's appointment disappeared after that first visit. Without a doubt we were fortunate to catch the cancer early and after surgery and numerous tests, the doctors pronounced me cancer free, although they recommended staying out of the sun as much as possible and making annual skin care checkups (which I do despite my aversion to doctor's offices).

Laird and I were still riding the wave of relief and joy from my favorable prognosis when, two months later, we discovered that I was pregnant. We were shocked and surprised since we had had trouble conceiving in the past and this baby was not planned. However, after the initial shock wore off, we were ecstatic. We believed God had delivered me from cancer and that He was further reaffirming LIFE by giving us another child. Well, you know the rest of the story. We lost this baby, our daughter Diandra, in our second miscarriage. Once again, my inner voice protested the unfairness of the situation. After all, we hadn't even asked for this child! At times it felt as if we were the victims of a cruel joke to be given the gift of a child only to have that gift ripped away.

For me and for many others who feel the unfairness of their loss, this feeling can easily translate into anger or rage. If this is your experience, you are not alone. I still vividly remember the first time I met Katherine. She had come up to talk to me after a seminar I had given on surviving miscarriage. What she had to say was poignant, intense, and reminded me so much of my own experience.

After our first miscarriage, I remember
standing outside looking up toward the sky
and screaming at God for taking our baby.

We had gone through so much trying to conceive. All those fertility treatments... I thought God was incredibly cruel for taking our baby after all we had been through. I finally got to the place where I wasn't feeling angry at God anymore. Then we had another miscarriage! I can't believe it happened again. Now I have these waves of anger and rage that just seem to hit me from out of the blue.

As with Katherine, every miscarriage survivor experiences anger at some point in his or her grieving process. The intensity and targets of this anger will vary from person to person. You may feel angry with...

❖ Family members and friends who have minimized your loss and your feelings.

❖ Strangers who have made insensitive comments about your baby's death.

❖ Your spouse for not feeling or expressing him/herself the same way you do.

❖ God for allowing such a tragedy to occur.

Some of you may have been taught that "anger is bad and anyone who allows himself to feel angry is sinning." This is an unfortunate misinterpretation of God's Word. Ephesians 4:26 says, "*Be angry* and sin not" (italics added). Anger, in and of itself, is NOT sinful. Scripture repeatedly acknowledges that anger is a normal human emotion. Jesus was **angry** when He cast the money changers from the temple. Throughout the Psalms, David sounds **angry** when he feels forsaken by God. Moses shattered the stone tablets in **anger** when he found his people making sacrifices to the golden calf. I believe God gave us these human and divine examples of anger in the Bible to illustrate that this emotion is both normal and natural. Once we experience anger we are faced with the choice of what to do with it.

It is not your emotion of anger that is sinful, it is the *unhealthy* or *inappropriate* expression of your anger that is sinful. In fact, your anger can be a helpful signal to let you know that something is wrong inside and needs your full attention. In my case, I needed to come to terms with the fact that life is not fair and that God does not promise us justice here on earth. I continually remind myself that *a child is a gift from God and not a reward for what I perceive as deserving behavior.*

Undoubtedly, your anger is painful. It can be damaging to you and the people you love only if you ignore it, act it out inappropriately, or allow it to explode. Used constructively, anger can be an ally in your healing process. The following exercises are intended to help you use your anger to heal.

EXERCISE 15: *Constructively Using Your Angry Energy*

If you are experiencing a lot of excess irritability and angry energy, you may need to physically exert yourself to release this tension. Some ideas of constructive physical activities are as follows:

✓ jogging	✓ washing your car
✓ fast walking	✓ washing windows
✓ swimming laps	✓ hitting your pillow
✓ aerobics	✓ thorough housecleaning

✓ reorganizing your garage
✓ kicking your beanbag chair
✓ yard work — mowing, raking, shoveling
✓ tearing up old magazines or phone books

✓ yelling in your car (windows rolled up)
✓ hitting baseballs at the batting cages
✓ playing a hard game of basketball or football
✓ hitting tennis balls against your garage door

EXERCISE 16: *Healing Through Words*

Another way of constructively venting your anger is through the written word. Writing has proven to be cathartic for many people.

FIRST: Take a few moments to focus on your anger. You can do this in a quiet room with your eyes closed. Identify the person/people with whom you are angry.

SECOND: Write a separate letter to each individual you have identified. Write about your anger using words and images powerful enough to accurately portray the intensity of your feelings. **Do not send these letters.** They are intended for your own private healing process. You may include these letters in your GRN if you are confident that they will not be read by anyone with whom you do not wish to share your thoughts and feelings.

If you find, as a result of this exercise, that you need to confront someone concerning your anger, use your letter to help you identify:

1. WHY are you angry? What did this person say or do to you? Try to be as specific as possible since this will help you determine what kind of resolution you are seeking.

2. WHAT do you want from this person now? An apology? A little understanding? Some compassion? A change in future behavior?

3. BEFORE confronting someone, determine an approach that is respectful to the other person. Confron-

tation which is destructive and blaming causes defensiveness thereby threatening the possibility of reconciliation. It is possible to be firm and expressive without being inappropriate. If this is difficult for you to do or if it seems like a particularly daunting task, ask for help from a friend, spouse, pastor, or counselor.

EXERCISE 17: Coloring Your Anger

If words do not come easily when you are angry, this exercise will help you express your feelings when your words simply fail to convey the fullness of your emotions. In this exercise, you are going to use color to symbolically express the feelings you have inside. *You do not need to be an artist to benefit from this exercise. Anything you create is right if it represents your anger.*

Suggested supplies:

- ✓ construction paper
- ✓ crayons
- ✓ finger paints
- ✓ colored pencils
- ✓ colored markers, etc.

I had a client once who tailored this exercise to her own personal style. She secured a large canvas in her garage and covered all her surrounding possessions with old sheets so they would be protected from any paint. Next she proceeded to soak old rags in buckets of a paint and water mixture and then throw the paint-soaked rags at her canvas with all her strength. She had a big smile on her face as she sat in my office the next day describing both her exhaustion and relief after her painting project was finished.

Whatever inventive method you choose, I recommend that you begin by finding a quiet place where you can complete this exercise uninterrupted. Close your eyes and concentrate on your anger. As those feelings come to the surface, use your crayons/paints to "color your anger." Your anger may express itself through the **movement** of the color across the page, in the **combination of colors** you choose, in a particular **shape or image**, or all of these possibilities. You can include your finished creation in your **GRN**.

Chapter Eight

COMMUNICATING YOUR NEEDS

"No one may forsake his neighbor when he is in trouble. Everybody is under obligation to help and support his neighbor as he would himself like to be helped."

— Martin Luther

When Laird and I lost our first baby, only four people even knew we were pregnant. During the initial weeks after the miscarriage, I really wanted to be left alone — to find my own way through my grief. I felt emotionally vulnerable around other people and, quite frankly, I don't think I trusted anyone with my pain. At that time, I was convinced that no one could really understand what I was going through. This changed, however, as the shock and trauma of our loss began to lessen. Then I found myself raw with a profound sadness and an overwhelming desire to talk with trusted friends — particularly women who had suffered a similar loss.

93

Many women have a similar reaction to mine, feeling unsure that anyone could truly comprehend the depths of their pain and yet yearning to be heard and understood. Megan, a support group member, was a good example of someone who had struggled and had triumphed over this inner conflict. She shared her emotional experience with me one evening after our group had ended.

> *I was really hesitant about coming to this group and talking to a bunch of strangers about something so personal. I just didn't think anyone would understand my pain. But there's a whole room full of people that know what I am going through and now I look forward to coming here every week. I never would have thought that I would* **want** *to talk about Mickey's death!*

Megan found her needs evolving as she traveled along her grief journey. You may find this true for you as well. Rarely, will your needs and feelings remain stagnant. Additionally, you may have physical as well as emotional needs as a consequence of your miscarriage since fatigue, insomnia, and anemia are common side effects of miscarriage.

Because of the unique emotional and physical aftermath you are suffering, you have special needs. Some of these needs you may have already addressed by working through Chapter Four with your spouse. However, you may also need things from friends and other family members.

Most miscarriage survivors would like support from their loved ones, but they feel exhausted and overwhelmed with the idea of trying to help each person understand their needs. Many friends and family members want to help, but some feel awkward about their role. Death is something our culture experiences with a great deal of uneasiness — especially the death of an innocent baby. Some people believe it is their responsibility to say the right thing, as if their words could take away the pain.

In fact, when I was asked to conduct an in-service training for the maternity nursing staff at a local hospital, I found that the majority of nurses felt very awkward and hesitant about dealing with a patient experiencing a still-birth or infant death. One nurse told me, "I chose this specialty because it's about LIFE — it's such a joy to help bring a baby into the world. I don't want to deal with death." Another nurse volunteered, "I'm always afraid I'll say the wrong thing. I don't really know what to say."

People who know I conduct seminars on miscarriage grief recovery often comment to me, "I really want to help my friend (or family member), but I just don't know what to say." Consequently, many well meaning and caring friends choose to say nothing at all. For a couple who has just lost a baby, this silence can be quite hurtful. Ironically, I find that the majority of miscarriage survivors just want their family and close friends to reach out with a simple heartfelt, "I'm so sorry about your loss." Miscarriage survivors do not expect people to say something to get rid of their pain. Sometimes family and friends just need a little guidance and then they are more than willing to support you in your time of grief.

I was fortunate that after my second miscarriage I had friends and family who understood my pain and loved me in very tangible ways. All I had to do was let my needs be known and voilá! There were wonderful women in my Bible study who organized two weeks of homemade meals for my family. Never have we eaten so well! Since I was sore all over and unable to lift Jordan, I had friends who gave freely of their time, babysitting so that I could get some much needed rest. There was also a group of women who hired a housecleaning service to give my house a thorough cleaning. (Since I had been so ill during my short-lived pregnancy, our house was a MESS and I had actually become quite depressed about it.) I was also incredibly grateful for those friends who were willing to listen to me talk about my miscarriage experience until I didn't need to talk about it anymore. It meant a great deal to me when friends would continue to ask about my emotional and physical health even past the first couple of weeks after my loss. Of course, we also got touching cards and beautiful floral arrangements that reminded us that we were not alone in our grief. Another poignant gesture was my sister's idea. She sent us some flowers a year later on the anniversary of Diandra's death as a way of letting us know that she still remembered our loss.

Perhaps trying to communicate your needs to others seems like a very unappealing and overwhelming task right now when you are in so much pain. However, I believe in most circumstances that it is well worth the effort. I felt so much support and caring from others after our second miscarriage. And I know that our friends felt better, too, because they were able to give and have their gifts (in whatever form) accepted. Don't you feel great when you give a gift that sincerely touches another person?

Consider using the exercises in this chapter to help your loved ones understand your special needs during this time of mourning. By giving them a sense of direction, *you will be equipping them to help you.*

EXERCISE 18: Identifying Your Needs

Here is a sample letter which includes a checklist of needs compiled by miscarriage survivors. Not all of the items will reflect your needs, but try to identify the items that do apply to you. Then use this letter and the needs you've identified to help you communicate with the people who want to help you. Giving friends and family some specific ideas increases the possibility of getting the kind of help you desire and avoiding the kind of help that you do not want.

Dear *{Insert Name}*,

As you know by now, I recently suffered a miscarriage. My precious baby is dead and I grieve for the child I will never hold in my arms, never rock to sleep, never kiss goodnight. At times the pain is so excruciating, it defies description.

I know that you care about me and that you want to help me in any way possible. Please understand if I withdraw from you. Sometimes I feel the need to be alone. Please be patient with me. There are things that you can do to help me as I cope with the loss of my baby.

- ❏ Visit me at home. Please call first.
- ❏ Ask if you can run any errands for me (shopping, carpooling, etc.)
- ❏ Ask if you can fix a meal for me and my family.
- ❏ Send a condolence card or flowers.
- ❏ Ask if you can help with household chores (laundry, housecleaning).
- ❏ Invite me out to do something. It would be nice to get out and have some fun.
- ❏ Be a good listener when I need to talk about my baby.

❏ Acknowledge that my miscarriage is a **death**.

❏ Respect my boundaries and try to understand when I need to be alone.

❏ Wait for me to call and make the first move.

❏ Commit to keeping me in your prayers on a regular basis.

❏ Don't try to find a reason for my miscarriage.

❏ Don't feel pressure to say the "right" thing. It doesn't exist.

❏ Understand that social interaction may be difficult for me.

❏ Please be sensitive to my emotional state especially at family gatherings and baby showers.

Please do NOT say any of the following:

{**Note: Although some of these statements may very well be true, inevitably they are experienced by grieving parents as hurtful.}

❖ "This is God's will"

❖ "You will have another baby"

❖ "You must have sin in your life and this is God's punishment"

❖ "Just be thankful for the children you do have"

❖ "A miscarriage is nature's way of sparing you a deformed child"

❖ "Don't be so sad. At least you didn't lose a **child**"

❖ "You're still young, you'll have another"

❖ "At least it happened now before you felt the baby moving (or before you bonded)"

❖ "Try to forget it and move on"

❑ Understand that silence is the worst thing to endure from my friends. Don't treat my miscarriage like a taboo subject, as if it never happened.

❑ Call me from time to time to see if I want to talk about my loss or about anything else.

[Adapted from the following sources: *Empty Arms*, Pam W. Vredevelt; *Coping with Miscarriage*, Dena K. Salmon; *Can We Prevent SIDS?*, Jennifer Cadoff; *Mom is Very Sick—Here's How to Help*, Wendy Bergren]

EXERCISE 19: Getting Help From A Friend

If communicating your needs to others seems too overwhelming to accomplish right now, you can get help from a friend. I was thankful to have some friends inquire about my needs and then organize a way to take care of those needs by assuming the responsibility for contacting other women to help.

Once you have used the checklist above to help you determine what you need from your loved ones, sit down with a close and trusted person and discuss these needs. Ask this person to communicate your needs to the rest of your loved ones so that you and your spouse are not deluged with telephone calls or other well-meaning, but unwanted, intrusions.

Chapter Nine

FOR SIBLINGS

"Oh, call my brother back to me!
I cannot play alone: The summer
comes with the flower and bee
— Where is my brother gone?"

— Felicia D. Hemmas

When I became pregnant the first time, Laird and I obviously did not have to deal with the issue of telling our other children about the pregnancy. Our second pregnancy was physically and emotionally difficult and demanding, but it ended in the safe and healthy delivery of our son, Jordan. When I became pregnant the third time, Jordan was only sixteen months old. We decided because of his age and the fact that young children do not understand time the same way adults do, we would wait until much later in the pregnancy before telling him. Consequently, he did not know about our second miscarriage at the time it occurred. Jordan is now five years old and we have explained to him about his baby sister who is living with God. From time to time he asks questions about her and I know it is still hard for him to completely comprehend the whole idea. (It's hard enough for us as adults!) During my fourth pregnancy, we again chose to wait until quite late in the pregnancy

before explaining to Jordan that he was going to have a
baby brother. By this time, Jordan was close to three and
he could see for himself that Mommy's tummy didn't look
the same. For us, this decision worked well because our
son did not have to endure an incredibly long wait for his
little brother to arrive.

When you and your spouse first found out you were
pregnant, you may have made a similar decision to wait
until you were further along in your pregnancy to tell your
other children. This is a popular decision, especially
among parents with small children. If this was the case in
your family, you may not need this chapter. *However, if
your children were told about your pregnancy, now you
must explain your miscarriage to them.* Be honest about
your feelings and your tears. Do not pretend everything
is fine when it is not. Children are rarely fooled. What
and how you tell them will depend upon their age and
maturity level.

Some preteens and most teenagers will understand the
concept of a miscarriage. You do not need to spell out
the graphic details for them and you do not need to force
your child to talk about his feelings. If you create an environment in which you are honest about expressing your
feelings constructively and you provide opportunities for
your child to express his feelings about the loss (some of
the exercises in this book on feelings and anger may be
appropriate for adolescents), he will feel safe to display his
own grief process. Also, keep in mind that some children
have a delayed reaction to miscarriage. They may begin
to show signs of grief months later.

It is a good idea for you to be prepared for your child
to have any combination of responses to your miscarriage.
Shanna was quite disturbed to find her three year-old
daughter playing "dead Barbies" shortly after Shanna's
son was stillborn.

I walked into the room and she had all her Barbies lying on the ground. She just kept saying, "You're dead," over and over. I got worried that now she's becoming obsessed with death.

While this kind of response can be upsetting for parents, Shanna's daughter was actually using play as a healthy outlet for her feelings. Young children will often use play to act out their feelings. Others will draw pictures or make clay sculptures. These are perfectly normal responses and you as parents can facilitate your children's healing process if you allow them to use their play in this manner. If you reach a point at which your child's play becomes worrisome to you, by all means contact a professional psychotherapist. He or she can evaluate your child and give you feedback as to whether or not the behavior is indicative of an abnormal grief reaction.

It is common, however, for siblings to experience confusion, fear, sadness, or anger after a miscarriage. Still other children may feel relief, guilt, or even happiness. (When a sibling experiences relief and/or happiness this may be an indication that your child had not yet accepted the idea of a baby brother or sister.) If you do not feel emotionally strong enough to deal with this kind of response from your child, ask a close friend or relative to help — or consider professional assistance.

Young children can be told that their baby sibling has gone to live with Jesus instead of coming home to live with the family. Explain that the baby was too sick to live on earth, but that she is in heaven living with Jesus and someday the family will see her. Again, be prepared for a variety of emotional responses, as well as questions about death and heaven. Young children may become fearful about dying. Reassure them that since they live **outside** of you, they can tell you when they are sick and you can take them to the doctor. Explain that it is much harder to know when a baby living **inside** of you is sick because she cannot talk and you cannot see her. I used this concept to write a fictionalized children's story to share with Jordan. Not only did this approach help him better understand his sister's death, but it also encouraged him to ask questions and discuss his feelings.

EXERCISE 20: *Goodbye Card/Picture*

Preschool and grade school children can benefit by saying goodbye to your baby in a homemade card or picture. Encourage them to use crayons, markers, and/or paint to create a special card or picture for the baby. Probably your children will want to dictate or write a short note to accompany the card. Include this card in your baby's scrapbook (see Chapter Twelve).

EXERCISE 21: *Feeling Picture*

Most children have not fully developed the skill of labeling their feelings with words. (Let's face it, many adults have difficulty doing this!) If you ask your child how she feels about your miscarriage, you may hear "I don't know." If you can sense (through your child's mood or behavior) that she has unresolved feelings about your miscarriage, encourage her to draw a picture of her feelings. After the picture is completed, ask open-ended questions such as, "tell me about this picture," to engage your child in a discussion. (Remember to practice your new listening skills with your children, too.)

If your child is reluctant or seems confused about how to draw a feeling picture, you may draw one first as an example (see Exercise 17 in Chapter Seven). Remember to share your feelings with your child as you talk about your finished work. Additionally, some parents are able to involve their hesitant child in a joint endeavor, drawing a picture together. In this case, use a large piece of paper and each of you may add your own special touches to your creation.

EXERCISE 22: Read Together

Fortunately there are a number of good books available today that are written especially for children coping with the concept of death. Find one and read it aloud with your child. Or write your own story and tailor it to the specific aspects involved in miscarriage. Remember to ask your child questions and to encourage his questions. I advise you to peruse any book prior to purchasing it to make sure that the author's treatment of the subject matches your own values and belief system. You can find these types of books at your local library, Christian bookstore, local bookstore, or through mail order catalogs. Turn to Appendix B for some suggestions.

Chapter Ten

GOD'S PROMISES

*"It appears that when life is broken by tragedy
God shines through the breach."*

— George A. Buttrick

After enduring the death of their baby, Beth and Daniel struggled to make sense of their conflicting feelings towards God. Beth felt immense comfort and peace. Her relationship with God was actually strengthened as a result of her tragedy. She found herself praying more, seeking God's comfort, and looking for His direction for her life. Daniel, on the other hand, felt abandoned by God. "Where was He when we needed Him?" he complained bitterly. Daniel was becoming cynical about his faith and he was pulling away from church and his Christian friends.

This difference in their feelings towards God greatly concerned Beth and Daniel, particularly since it was a new development in their relationship. It was for this reason they came to me for marriage counseling. Beth was both worried and angry about Daniel's growing resentment toward God. Daniel was annoyed by Beth's lack of understanding and what he called her Pollyanna attitude.

Using the empathic listening skills discussed in Chapter Four, I worked to help Beth and Daniel better understand each other's feelings and to better communicate their own respective feelings and needs. Eventually, Beth and Daniel were able to see that it is not necessary for both partners to have the *same* feelings (in fact, it is inevitable that at some point they will not). It is only necessary to try to communicate effectively, to try to understand the other person, and to offer emotional support. At this point, Beth began to try to support Daniel's grieving process rather than nagging him to choose her healing path. She gave him the freedom to work through his anger in his way and at his pace (as long as he agreed to express his anger appropriately). She even confronted her own fears about Daniel's feelings towards God, admitting that she was afraid Daniel would abandon his faith forever. Daniel readily admitted that he wished he could have Beth's attitude towards God. He actually felt a little envious of her, but his anger was standing in the way of his reconciliation with God. He agreed to deal directly with his anger by completing the exercises in this book and by discussing his feelings in our counseling sessions. Once he did this, Daniel was ready to reapproach God. I suggested that he start by reading his Bible and claiming God's promises.

As Daniel worked to put words to his feelings, he discovered that because he felt abandoned by the very God he had trusted with his child's precious life, he was extremely angry. He wanted to withdraw from God because he felt betrayed. Perhaps you feel this way too. You are certainly not alone. One of the things I appreciated knowing when I was grieving was that even a great spiritual scholar and writer like C.S. Lewis felt anger and abandonment at his time of loss. C.S. Lewis married later in his life and tragically lost his wife after they had spent only a short time together. After the death of his beloved spouse, he wrote about his despair.

Meanwhile, where is God? This is one
of the most disquieting symptoms. When
you are happy, so happy that you have no
sense of needing Him, if you turn to Him
then with praise, you will be welcomed with
open arms. But go to Him when your need
is desperate, when all other help is vain and
what do you find? A door slammed in your
face, and a sound of bolting and double bolting on the inside. After that, silence. You
may as well turn away.

A Grief Observed

I, too, felt alone and alienated from God during the
initial phases of my grief. After Diandra's death, I received numerous sympathy cards with Bible verses in-
serted in them. But, I felt so abandoned by God that I
had an extremely hard time reading and appreciating
God's comforting Word. Instead of feeling peace, I felt
anger. Then Laird and I received a card from friends
with a handwritten note from the wife. She explained
that after her miscarriage, a particular passage from C.S.
Lewis' book, *The Magician's Nephew* (one of the books
in *The Chronicles of Narnia* series) was particularly helpful to her and she included it for us to read. In spite of my
initial cynicism that any words could penetrate my grief-
stricken soul, I was deeply moved by this story and its
message. I include it in this book with the hope that it
may touch someone else's heart with the same compassion in which it touched mine.

In this story, a young boy named Digory is afraid because his mother is ill and he is beginning to realize that
she is going to die. In the midst of his grief, he meets
Aslan the Lion (the Christ figure in these Chronicles).
Aslan asks Digory to help Him with a dangerous task....

"I asked, are you ready," said the Lion.

"Yes," answered Digory. He had had for a second some wild idea of saying, "I'll help you if you promise to help about my mother," but he realized in time that the Lion was not at all the sort of person one could try to make bargains with. But when he had said, "Yes," he thought of his mother, and he thought of the great hopes he had had and how they were all dying away and a lump came in his throat and tears in his eyes, and he blurted out:

"But please, please — won't you — can't you give me something that will cure my mother?" Up till then he had been looking at the Lion's great front feet and the huge claws on them; now, in his despair, he looked up at its face. What he saw surprised him as much as anything in his whole life. For the tawny face was bent down near his own and (wonder of wonders) great shining tears stood in the Lion's eyes. They were such big, bright tears compared with Digory's own that for a moment he felt as if the Lion must really be sorrier about his mother than he himself.

"My son, my son," said Aslan. "I know. Grief is great...."

It is easy to forget that God knows and understands our grief in a very intimate and personal way. I found myself at one point crying out to God, "I lost my daughter!" — as if He could never fathom the depth of my pain.

And yet He willingly surrendered His very own Son for me and for you with full knowledge of the rejection and crucifixion Jesus would endure. I believe that God is truly grieved every time a person rejects His Son and the only path to eternal life. He created each and every one of us and I do not believe that He wants to lose any of us to everlasting alienation from Him.

If you allow God to speak to you through His Word, the Bible can be a great source of comfort and peace in the midst of your grief. You hold the key to the door and it is your choice as to whether or not you will let God in to become a partner in your pain. This choice can be very difficult when you are suffering tremendous hurt and perhaps even doubting God's love and concern for your personal circumstance. Scriptures tell us that He will never leave nor forsake His children. God has given us many Bible promises to sustain us during troubled times. Perhaps some of the following references will speak to you in your time of need.

EXERCISE 23: Claiming God's Promises

Have you ever had the experience of sitting in the church congregation on a Sunday morning feeling certain that the pastor had peeked into your life and constructed his sermon just for you? Although God's Word is applicable to everyone's life, I believe there are times He uses certain Scripture to speak specifically to particular people in need. Look up the following references in your Bible. Read each one and on a separate piece of paper write God's promise or reassurance to you. Include these promises in your GRN.

James 1:2-4	Psalm 34:18,19
Deuteronomy 31:6	II Corinthians 4:8-9, 16-17
I Peter 1:6-7	II Corinthians 1:8-10

John 9:1-3	Isaiah 40:29-31
Romans 8:28	Isaiah 61:3
Romans 5:3-5	II Kings 20:5
II Corinthians 1:3-5	Psalm 9:9-10
Isaiah 43:2	Jeremiah 29:11

EXERCISE 24: Scripture Meditation

The preceding exercise was meant to give you a small sampling of Bible verses to help you understand God's promises to you in time of need. You may find other Bible verses or passages from books (such as the passage from *The Magician's Nephew*) that have special meaning for you. Make up 3 x 5 cards for each verse that has a special meaning for you during this time of grief and healing. Place these cards in strategic areas of your home, car, or workplace to encourage you to meditate on God's Word.

Chapter Eleven

MEETING YOUR BABY

"We watch'd her breathing through the night,
her breathing soft and low,
as in her breath the wave of life
kept heaving to and fro."

— Thomas Hood

ometimes I meet with resistance when I encourage hurting parents to use their imagination to visualize their lost baby. Marcy was a support group member who initially balked at this idea, sharing her reservations aloud with the rest of the group.

I don't really want to do this. Can I skip
this part? Why do we need to pick a name,
anyway? I mean, it's not like it looked like
*a **real** baby.*

Those parents who suffered a stillbirth are sometimes constrained by their memories of how their lifeless child looked and felt as they held her for the first and last time. Then there are those, like Marcy, who remember seeing clumps of fetal tissue that looked nothing like a baby. This was also the case for Laird and me when we suffered our first miscarriage and had to scoop up strange looking remains to take to the doctor's office for lab analysis. I still remember sitting in my obstetrician's waiting room, tightly holding a small plastic container with my baby's remains inside, surrounded by obviously pregnant women comparing notes about food cravings, in utero baby hiccups, and frequent trips to the bathroom! However, when I think about our first child, whom we named Jared because we just felt in our hearts that he was a boy, I do not imagine clumps of fetal tissue. I use my imagination to picture him as a healthy baby and I avoid being bound by the reality of what I carried in that plastic container.

Perhaps you are one of those parents who actually saw a fully formed fetus that did not yet resemble your expectation of your own sweet Gerber baby. When I had labor induced to deliver our daughter Diandra, I was ambivalent about whether or not I wanted to see her when she was delivered. Quite frankly, I was frightened about what I might see. I didn't know if she was going to look like a baby — if she was going to be terribly deformed — if she was going to come out in pieces. I finally decided that I wanted to see her, regardless of her condition, because she was my baby and maybe there was something more I could learn about her if I looked at her. We had only a short time together after she was delivered and my worst fears never materialized. She was a whole, tiny baby — despite appearing incredibly fragile. She was fifteen weeks old (gestational age) and she looked like the pictures of fetuses that I had seen in books. She did not yet look like a full term infant or have any distinctive physical features that might suggest a resemblance to a particular family member or allow me to speculate about a certain personality. But, there was no mistaking that she was a human being.

Although you may have some initial resistance to the idea of imagining your baby, do not let your mind sabotage your healing process by blocking your creativity. Research indicates that the majority of women envision a **baby** (not an embryo or fetus) from the moment they find out they are pregnant. When my first pregnancy was confirmed, I immediately began envisioning a real baby in my mind. This wasn't a conscious choice on my part — the images just spontaneously occurred in my mind's eye. I could even leaf through a parenting magazine and find pictures of babies that bore a remarkable resemblance to the image I entertained of my own baby. And the same thing happened when I watched television! Some of those kids in commercials appeared to me as if they could have been mine.

Imagining what your unborn child would have looked liked really isn't so hard to do. We know what we look like and most of us know what our extended biological family members look like. It is just a short jump in imagination to factor these things together and come up with an image. I ended up saving a few of those magazine pictures after our first miscarriage and after Jordan's birth I found that there was an amazing resemblance between two of those pictures and my real life son!

Meeting your baby as a real person involves allowing your mind to take the knowledge you do have about your child and to enhance it into a meaningful image for you. Why should you do this? First, meeting your baby *validates your loss* as significant and profound because you attach the loss to the visual image of your *baby*. You are not trying to mourn a clump of fetal tissue or a faceless, nameless fetus, but a human being! Second, once you have made your baby's image concrete, you begin to *understand the prenatal bonding* that had already occurred and that many people deny. Third, meeting your baby is a *prerequisite to saying goodbye* to your child. It is almost impossible to say goodbye to a baby that is a shapeless, nameless, lump of tissue.

EXERCISE 25: Visualizing Your Baby

FIRST:

Find a quiet place where you can complete this exercise uninterrupted. Find a relaxed body position and close your eyes. Imagine your baby as an actual infant and visually memorize his or her physical description. If this is difficult for you, use the dreams and images you experienced when you found out you were pregnant. After you have a complete image, describe your baby by using the questions below as aids.

- ❖ Gender?
- ❖ Name? (Choose a name if you haven't already.)
- ❖ Hair color?
- ❖ Eye color?
- ❖ Complexion?
- ❖ Other physical attributes?
- ❖ Any family resemblances?
- ❖ If yes, to whom and in what way?

SECOND:

Option #1: Keeping the image of your baby in mind, draw a picture of your child. Use pen, pencils, crayons, paints, and construction paper as desired.

Option #2: For those of you who are uncomfortable with your drawing ability, find a picture/s in a baby or parent magazine that matches your image of your baby and paste it in your grief recovery notebook. (Caution: Sifting through pictures of babies will stir up your emotions.)

EXERCISE 26: Hello Letter

Write a hello letter to your baby. Express your love, the plans you had for his future. Describe yourself, your spouse, and any of the baby's siblings to him. Let your child know how you were preparing for his arrival — nursery, toys, etc.

This is also a healing exercise for grieving siblings to participate in since it helps them release their feelings by providing both focus and structure. You might consider making this exercise a family project with each member contributing a part of the letter.

Chapter Twelve

SAYING GOODBYE

"Love has a hundred gentle ends."

— Leonora Speyer

t was a sunny and warm summer day, but my heart was heavy with grief. We had recently lost our daughter, Diandra, and I was driving home from work with her image in my mind. For some reason I always picture our daughter as a toddler with blonde curls, crystal blue eyes, a mischievous smile, and a delightful giggle. As I struggled with that huge emptiness in my heart, I began to talk to her. I told her about her daddy, her big brother Jordan, her mommy, and how much we all loved her and would miss her. I shared with her the sadness I felt that we would never be able to do mother-daughter activities together. While I was talking, I realized I was saying goodbye. I talked and wept and finally let go. I pictured myself putting my baby girl back in Jesus' arms. As I said goodbye for the last time, I could swear that I heard this soft, high-pitched voice in my mind say, "Bye-bye, Mama."

You have traveled a long way in your healing process and you are now nearing the final path of this journey. It is time to say goodbye to your baby. Although this will be painful, it is time for you to entrust your baby to Jesus.

I never thought I would be able to say goodbye to my baby. I thought that saying goodbye meant I couldn't think about her or talk about her. I thought you were going to ask me to erase her from my mind as if she never existed.

But, that wasn't how it was at all. Saying goodbye was really hard, but you encouraged us to think about our babies being with Jesus and remembering things about them that could bring us joy and comfort. I treasure the brief memories of my daughter. I look forward to knowing her in heaven someday. (Like you said, she's in heavenly arms now!) I think I'm ready to move on...

I received this letter from Rebecca after she attended my workshop for miscarriage survivors. She writes about a fear that many parents have when they are faced with the idea of saying goodbye to their child. "Does this mean I pretend that my baby never existed?" Absolutely NOT! Sometimes it is easier to think about saying goodbye to your baby if you think about saying goodbye to a very dear friend who is moving to another continent and you both know in your hearts that you will not see each other again on this earth. Does that mean you forget about your friend? Do you erase all memories of her from your mind? No. You keep your treasured memories, while accepting the reality of the separation. If you ruminate over this separation, you will not be able to get on with your life. It is a similar process when you say goodbye to your baby. You must not let your memories of the miscarriage and the dreams of what "could have been" prevent you from living life. Too many people miss the blessings of the present because they are living in the past. This is why you must let go — to refocus your energy so that you are able to live in the present. This is the last healing step.

Saying goodbye is a very personal and poignant experience. The following exercises are suggestions which other grieving parents have found helpful. The most important thing for you to do is to say a goodbye that is meaningful to you and these ideas should help you do that.

EXERCISE 27: Goodbye Letter

Just as you wrote a hello letter to your baby in the previous chapter, it is now time to say goodbye. You can write about your sadness, describing the things you will miss doing, learning, and exploring together. Describe her "new" home (heaven) to her and explain that you will see her again someday.

This exercise also works well with sibling loss. Ask your child if he is interested in writing (or dictating, if he can't write yet) a goodbye letter to his baby brother or sister.

A nice variation of this idea is to write a poem or short story in which you say your goodbye in a manner that is significant to you.

EXERCISE 28: Giving Your Baby to Jesus

This is a powerful exercise which calls on you to use your creativity through visualization (the process of picturing images in your mind). Occasionally, some people are wary of this process primarily because they misunderstand it. This is not hypnotism and throughout this exercise you will maintain complete control over your thoughts and images. You will use visualization to give your baby to the only person who could love him and care for him better than you could — Jesus.

Find a quiet place where you can complete this exercise without interruption. Relax your body and close your eyes. Picture yourself rocking your baby in a rocking chair. Tell your baby how much you love him and how much you will miss him. Explain that you must say goodbye now because Jesus has come to take him home to heaven. Look up and see Jesus walking towards you, arms outstretched. Picture yourself placing your infant in Jesus' loving arms. Give him one last kiss and loving embrace. Watch as Jesus walks away and carries him through the gates of heaven. Be assured in your heart that your baby is safe and loved.

EXERCISE 29: Memorial Service

Hold a formal or informal memorial service for family and friends. This gives you the opportunity to say goodbye with the support of your family and friends present. It also gives your loved ones a chance to say their own goodbyes to your baby, so everyone can experience some sense of closure. You and your spouse may wish to speak about your feelings and the dreams you had for your baby. You may want to share the letters you have written to your baby. Also, you may choose to have a pastor present to share from God's word or offer a prayer for you.

EXERCISE 30: Plant a Tree

When Jordan and Carson were born we planted a tree for each of them in my parents' yard (our yard was too small for any additions). We like the idea of watching the trees mirror the growth of our sons. Although our trees are for our living children, some people find that planting a tree for their lost child is also rewarding. Perhaps for some of you, a daily reminder of your child would be too painful. On the other hand, many of you may find something poignant and hopeful about having a living symbol of your baby. You can plant a tree in your yard as a living memorial to the baby you lost. *This can help you remember that your child is thriving in heaven.*

EXERCISE 31: *Make a Scrapbook*

To honor your baby's memory, make a scrapbook or scrapbox filled with mementos. Over the years, I have seen some very beautiful memory boxes made by the people in my Empty Arms groups. It is easy to see the love that went into these efforts to remember their lost children.

As a variation of this idea, you can turn your scrapbook into an excellent family project. In this way, each family member has a chance to participate, contributing something special to the scrapbook/box as a personal way of saying goodbye. Grieving together as a family can facilitate the healing process by decreasing the sense of isolation and increasing emotional intimacy. The possibilities of items to include in your scrapbook are numerous. Some suggestions are as follows:

- ❖ sonogram picture of your baby in utero
- ❖ home pregnancy test stick
- ❖ booties grandma had knitted
- ❖ blanket you embroidered
- ❖ special toy you bought
- ❖ scrap of the wallpaper from the nursery
- ❖ your letters to your baby

124 In Heavenly Arms

- ❖ your children's letters/cards/pictures to the baby
- ❖ condolence cards you received
- ❖ dried flowers from bouquets you received
- ❖ hometown newspaper to show what was happening in the world and your town
- ❖ pictures from your baby shower

EXERCISE 32: *Giving to Others*

While saving one or two of the special things you purchased or made for your baby can be healing (as in EXERCISE 31), holding onto all of these things can inhibit the letting go process. You may want to consider giving some of your baby's things to charity. This act of giving to others will help you acknowledge that your baby is gone. It can also bring a lot of joy to children whose parents cannot provide for them.

It is important to exercise caution if you choose to give to others. Giving away every reminder of your baby can plunge you into denial and hurt your recovery process. Additionally, you may need those baby things for your next child (if you intend to try again and God blesses you), so that giving them away would be an impractical choice right now. Consider all of these aspects and work toward a balanced decision concerning giving to others.

EXERCISE 33: *Balloon Ceremony*

This ceremony is one of my favorite features of our Empty Arms group. Saying goodbye can be such a painful and dreaded experience, but we have found that members are truly moved and comforted by this poignant ceremony. Almost every group participant has positive comments to make about the balloons!

Prior to the seventh session, the group facilitator purchases a number of helium filled balloons with ribbons attached. We provide one balloon for each child lost. Some people like to use pink or blue balloons to represent the gender of their lost child, but we choose white for the symbolism of purity and innocence. Then we take some time during our group session to write a goodbye note on a 3 x 5 card and attach it to the ribbon on the balloon. When everyone is ready, we step outside into the night and release the balloons into the sky as a visual symbol of releasing our children to God in heaven. The white balloons create a beautiful, luminescent sight against the night sky as they float away carrying our messages of love.

EXERCISE 34: *Christmas Ornament*

Christmas can be a difficult time for grieving parents. The pain of your loss may be exacerbated as your family members (including pregnant relatives, young children, and babies) come together to celebrate the joy of Christ's birth. Perhaps you will find the idea of celebrating the birth of an infant boy (Jesus Christ) brings you face to face with your own empty cradle.

Oftentimes, family members and friends also feel awkward about how to handle your loss. Should they send you a Christmas card with their family picture in it? Should they invite you to their Christmas open house, knowing there will be kids and babies present? Should they acknowledge your loss or remain silent? You may want to review Chapter Eight and consider a way to communicate your desires in this area.

There is hope for surviving the holidays after your loss. I have watched grieving parents in my Empty Arms support group triumph over their pain during the Christmas season. One woman found an exquisite angel ornament that she felt symbolized her lost baby and she hung it on her Christmas tree as a reminder of the family's "angel in heaven." This way her baby could still be a part of their family traditions and celebrations in a symbolic way. She shared this idea with other members, and it caught on! (I myself own several angel ornaments — many of them gifts from group members.) Consider purchasing or making your own angel (or teddy bear or anything else that reminds you of your baby) ornament and starting a new tradition in your home.

EXERCISE 35: Write a Song

I still vividly remember the day that I heard on the news that Eric Clapton's young son had fallen to his death from the window of his highrise apartment. I can only imagine the immense grief his parents must have suffered. Sometime later, Eric Clapton used his musical talent to help him express his grief and to say goodbye to his beloved son. Below is an excerpt from his song, Tears in Heaven.

> Would you know my name if I saw you in heaven?
> Would it be the same if I saw you in heaven?
> I must be strong and carry on
> 'cause I know I don't belong here in heaven....
>
> Beyond the door, there's peace I'm sure.
> And I know there'll be no more tears in heaven....
>
> — Eric Clapton

You don't have to be a grammy-winning recording artist to benefit from this exercise. In fact, I had a very musically gifted client whose grief recovery process was accelerated by a day spent at her keyboard. She wrote several lullabies and songs for her lost son as a way of sharing her feelings and healing her pain. I thought this was a wonderfully sensitive and personal way of saying goodbye. If you are musically inclined, you may also find this idea particularly appealing.

Chapter Thirteen

PREGNANT AGAIN

"Hope without risk is not hope."

— *Dom Helder Camara*

rankly, trying to get pregnant again after each of our miscarriages was a big hassle. Our sex life became a series of well-orchestrated events dictated by the charts in which I faithfully recorded my basal body temperature, PMS symptoms, and mucus consistencies. It got to the point that Laird would groan audibly when I sent him off to work in the morning saying, "Tonight's the night!" It's amazing how mandatory sex can take all the pleasure (well, a lot of the pleasure) out of the experience! Also, time seemed to pass so slowly and it seemed as if we were always waiting. Waiting for the right time to try to conceive.... Waiting to see if my period was late so I could take another home pregnancy test....Testing negative and waiting to try again. Every month that passed without successful conception was like a precious month lost. Both Laird and I had to battle against our discouragement and frustration. For me, I also struggled with nagging doubts. After my first miscarriage I had doubts that I would ever be a mother. I wondered if I would ever know what it was like to hold my own baby in my arms. After our second miscarriage, I began to doubt whether

Jordan would ever have a sibling. He is such a loving, extroverted child that we wanted a little brother or sister for him as well as for ourselves.

Eventually, I became pregnant again and a whole new emotional roller coaster ride began. Every time I felt elation, it was immediately followed by apprehension. When I felt excitement, fear stiffled it. Through the first four months of my pregnancies, I was not able to allow myself to really enjoy the reality of a child growing inside my womb. Guarded is a good way to describe my emotional state during that time. Some of this guardedness was due to my hyperemesis and my spotting and cramping problems. But some of my attitude was due to a natural reflex experienced by miscarriage survivors. If this emotional process sounds familiar, it is because you are trying to protect yourself from further pain by postponing the bonding process — in a sense, trying hard not to let the pregnancy become too real. And if you, like me, experienced cramping or bleeding in a pregnancy following a miscarriage, you were probably filled with dread and apprehension because, in your mind, blood equals miscarriage. Fortunately, this is not always the case. Many women spot during their pregnancies and still deliver healthy, full term babies. Of course, you should always report spotting and cramping symptoms to your physician and he or she will advise you.

Undeniably, getting pregnant again after a miscarriage or stillbirth can feel like stumbling through a maze of confusing and even conflicting emotions. Fear and apprehension may be your constant companions. It is frightening to think that you could lose another baby. And it is often equally frightening to think about allowing yourself to feel excitement about the new life growing inside of you. You will find that every day is an exercise of your faith in God — particularly until you pass that **critical**

point (the point at which you lost your last child). Your anxiety and apprehension are normal, natural reactions because you are trying to protect yourself from further pain. There are no magic exercises I can suggest that will make those unpleasant feelings disappear. Some of you will be able to give your feelings to God and be done with them. For others of you, you will work to find a way to live with your feelings without letting them overtake you. Laird and I found that our feelings of apprehension and our guarded attitude remained with us for quite some time despite our prayers that God would free us of our concerns. Perhaps this was because of insufficient faith on our part. I prefer to believe that God had a purpose in allowing us to experience those feelings, part of which may have been to force us to find constructive ways to help us cope with our emotions. I want to share with you some of the things that allayed our anxiety as we found ourselves pregnant again. You may also find it helpful to consider some of the following suggestions:

GET EARLY PRENATAL CARE!

Make sure you let your doctor know your obstetrics history. Sometimes this may require you to be insistent when you schedule your initial prenatal visit over the phone since many receptionists are trained to schedule visits at particular gestational milestones. For example, it is my obstetrician's policy to schedule her patients' first prenatal appointment with the nurse practitoner (rather than the doctor) eight weeks into the pregnancy. This may be fine for the majority of women who have normal pregnancies, but for someone with miscarriages and hyperemesis in her obstetrics history this policy felt inadequate to me. So I asked to speak to the doctor and we made alternate arrangements more appropriate for my needs. Most caring doctors will take extra precautions and care with a woman who has a history of miscarriage. (Some doctors will not consider you a high risk pregnancy if you have had less than three miscarriages. Even if you have only had one miscarriage, find a doctor who is sensitive to your loss and is willing to take the extra time and precautions you want.)

During your initial visit with your doctor, you may want to discuss the kinds of precautions and preventative treatments that are recommended for certain women with a miscarriage history. I know from my own experience that a simple blood test can rule out a number of medial conditions that may predispose a woman to miscarriage. Such conditions may include, but are not necessarily limited to:

✧ Low progesterone levels - Progesterone is a hormone that plays a significant role in preparing the uterus for the implantation and development of the fertilized ovum. Progesterone supplements are sometimes prescribed during the first trimester for women who have a miscarriage history or who have low levels of this hormone. Typically a blood panel is ordered for every pregnant woman at the time of her initial prenatal visit. Ask your doctor to test your progesterone levels at this time and review with him or her the merits of supplements for your particular case. I used progesterone supplements during my first trimester with Jordan, but I did not use progesterone during my pregnancy with Carson and both pregnancies were successful. I did not, however, use progesterone during any of my pregnancies that ended in miscarriage.

✧ Thyroid problems - The thyroid is a gland located in the neck which secretes the hormones, thryroxine, tri-iodothyronine, and calcitonin. These hormones, in turn, regulate body growth, calcium levels, and metabolism.

According to my doctors, undiagnosed thyroid conditions are common in women and sometimes these problems contribute to miscarriage.

✦ Lupus - There are different forms of this chronic disease which is an autoimmune disorder affecting connective tissue and possibly other systems in the body. This disease affects nine times as many women as men, and frequently strikes women of childbearing age. Some characteristics of this disorder have been associated with miscarriage.

✦ Diabetes - a disorder in which the pancreas produces little or no insulin. When my doctor decided to rule out possible complicating factors in my pregnancies, diabetes was on the list. Thankfully, I tested negative. If you are a known diabetic, please consult with your obstetrician prior to becoming pregnant so that your doctor has an opportunity to monitor closely all aspects of your health and high-risk pregnancy.

✦ Anemia - a condition in which the hemoglobin in the blood is below normal levels. One of the most common causes of anemia is iron deficiency. While anemia is a common physical consequence of miscarriage, some doctors speculate that an anemic condition prior to miscarriage can put the pregnancy at risk.

This list of disorders is not meant in any way to be a diagnosis or explanation of your particular miscarriage history. Please understand that I am not a medical doctor. I share this list with you because these were the conditions that my doctor suggested we rule out in my situation. *Always discuss your individual circumstance and health history with your own doctor.* You may also want to find out what your doctor has to say about exercise and intercourse during your first trimester when your risk for miscarriage is at its highest. Some doctors take a conservative position, restricting these types of activities until the health of the fetus is secure.

Regardless of the specifics of your case, always keep the lines of communication open with your doctor. Talk about your fears and be sure to report any bleeding, spotting, cramping, or other unusual physical sensations as soon as they occur. Your doctor can educate you about the kinds of physical symptoms that are considered normal in pregnancy so that you will be able to identify anything unusual. Just ask! Also, there are several good books about pregnancy that are available at your local bookstore. Consider purchasing one to have on hand as an in-home resource. My best advice to you if you have **any doubts** about your pregnancy is to call your doctor and discuss your symptoms as soon as possible.

Additionally, some obstetricians will authorize an early ultrasound to put your mind at ease about your baby's development. Laird and I were unable to get our insurance company to pay for a second ultrasound on Carson (we had already used our only authorized sonogram early in the pregnancy when I was cramping and spotting), but we chose to incur the out-of-pocket expense for our own peace of mind. We wanted to make sure his development was normal, particularly in light of our previous second trimester miscarriage and because I had had hyperemesis during my pregnancy with Carson. We both felt that the ultrasound was well worth the additional expense.

Asking questions and gaining knowledge are great ways to combat anxiety. Above all — be assertive with your needs. If you feel you are not getting the kind of medical attention you desire, switch doctors. There are plenty of competent and empathic doctors available.

HAVE A PLAN ABOUT SHARING THE NEWS OF YOUR PREGNANCY

Laird and I actually had a plan about how we would share our news when we became pregnant the very first time. We opted to take the cautious route, telling the majority of our friends and coworkers after the third month. (Of course, we didn't get that far the first time. But we were relieved that we didn't have to inform a whole legion of people about our miscarriage since we had not shared our news with a lot of people in the beginning.)

Soon after you discover you are pregnant, you and your spouse should sit down and decide how, when, and with whom to share the news of your pregnancy. Many couples who have survived miscarriage decide to wait until after the **critical point** to share their news. Others desire the prayer and emotional support from as many people as possible, so they choose to share their good news immediately. Additionally, you may elect to consider the feelings of close friends and family members as you make this decision. Sometimes loved ones may hear about your miscarriage (particularly if a medical procedure is involved) before they have been told about your pregnancy. Often this leaves family members feeling hurt and left out. In any case, it is important to remember that there is not just one right way to share the news of your pregnancy. Since every situation is unique, I recommend that you follow your heart and God's leading so that you can be confident that your choice is the best one for you.

PRAY TOGETHER

Some of our best moments of emotional and spiritual intimacy have come when Laird and I have prayed together about our pregnancies. I felt immense comfort when Laird would place his hand over my growing mid-section and pray for our baby's safe and healthy develop-ment and delivery. Many people I work with have men-tioned the benefits to both their marriage and to their peace of mind regarding their pregnancies when they pray with their partner. You and your spouse can also bring your fears and hopes to God in prayer. Pray for a safe and normal pregnancy; a healthy, full term baby; compe-tent medical care; God's comfort and peace in times of apprehension; and a deepening and strengthening of your marital relationship.

Chapter Fourteen

SPECIAL CIRCUMSTANCES

*"Man has ever risen near to God
by the altar stairs of pain and sorrow."*

— S.A. Adler

Every time that Judy began to share in her support group, she began to cry. This is not at all unusual. She and her husband had just suffered their fifth miscarriage and they were also dealing with special challenges in conceiving. Judy's support group facilitator had also noticed that Judy always stayed after group to talk and that she phoned the facilitator frequently during the week. It was clear to this leader that Judy was experiencing complicated bereavement due to multiple miscarriages and infertility problems. This simply means that Judy's grief was compounded by other special circumstances and that she could benefit from some additional support. Her group leader had referred her to me for some individual grief counseling. This did NOT mean Judy was weak or crazy. It only meant that Judy's grief was intense and profound. It was interfering with her ability to function daily and her support group, while very helpful, was not quite enough to help Judy cope with her pain. Judy made remarkable progress in her healing process after she added short-term grief counseling to her schedule.

Maryanne had been diagnosed by her doctor as pre-menopausal. She was forty-two years old and her menstrual cycles were very sporadic and unpredictable. She and her husband, Sam, had been married three years and they had been trying to conceive ever since saying, "I do." Maryanne was distraught as she sat on the couch in my office for the first time. In between sobs she explained her reason for coming to see me.

> *Sam thinks I'm crazy for even coming to counseling. He would never come. He doesn't think it's necesary.... Ever since I can remember, my cycle has been as regular as clockwork. 31 days. Always 31 days. Martin, my first husband never wanted children and it just didn't seem so important to me back then. I guess I thought I could get pregnant any time I really wanted to, so I was never concerned about it. Now my desire to have kids is so strong and I'm running out of time. Sam is kind of indifferent about the whole thing. I think he likes his life the way it is and kids would just change things too much. When I had my miscarriage, he was aloof about the whole thing. I remember him saying, "Well, maybe this is for the best. We are pretty set in our life style." It's kind of hard to cope with my feelings about the miscarriage and this "pre-menopausal" thing — whatever that means. The doctor said my body's getting ready for the change and my hormone changes are*

*affecting my cycle. It's totally unpredictable.
I went three months without any period! I
don't stand a chance of getting pregnant if I
can't even predict when I'm ovulating. The
doctor says we can do all this fancy and ex-
pensive stuff for infertility, but Sam is against
it because he says we need to just "let what's
going to happen, happen."*

It was evident that Maryanne was distressed for a
number of reasons. She had unresolved grief from her
miscarriage, infertility problems, an unsupportive spouse,
and time was her enemy. She and Sam were not in agreement about the parenthood decision and this created
more conflict between them. Maryanne was definitely
an excellent candidate for some individual counseling because her situation was complex and unlikely to improve
without some professional intervention.

Sophie was another client of mine who was dealing
with complicated bereavement issues surrounding her
miscarriage. After her first-trimester miscarriage, her
physician assured her that her prospects for conceiving
and carrying a baby to term were excellent because she
was young and healthy. However, Sophie was having
great difficulty finding and holding on to the hope of ever
being a parent because she was preoccupied with the re-
cent death of her own parent. Evidently, Sophie and her
husband, Edward, found out they were pregnant about a
week after Sophie's mother had died of a heart attack.
The mother had no known history of heart disease and
her death came as quite a shock to the entire family. For
Sophie her mother's death created an additional emotional dilemma. She wanted to be happy about her pregnancy, but since her mother had just died, she felt that joy
and excitement were inappropriate emotions to feel, much
less express. As a result, Sophie was unable to explore

her feelings about being pregnant and she was also unable to grieve her mother's death in a way that brought true healing. Currently exacerbating this existing emotional conflict was the new pain from her miscarriage. As a result, Sophie was carrying a huge burden of confused, intense, and unexpressed feelings.

This book is intended to facilitate your grieving and healing process. As I mentioned previously, grief is complicated and it can take a long time to work through. You may feel that these exercises do not adequately deal with the depth and extent of your pain just as Judy, Maryanne, and Sophie discovered that they needed more than their support groups to help them heal. Also, some people are uncomfortable with group process and they simply prefer the privacy that individual counseling provides. These are common experiences. If you are dealing with any or all of the special circumstances listed in this chapter, it is likely that you will want to consider assistance beyond this book. Trust your instincts and seek out the help you need to heal.

Examples of special circumstances causing complicated bereavement could include, but are not limited to the following:

❖ Multiple miscarriages

❖ Infertility

❖ Menopausal pregnancy

❖ No spouse or unsupportive spouse

❖ Unresolved grief from other deaths

If any of the above special situations describe you, you may want to consider some additional assistance. Please know that there are people who want to help you. Detailed on the following pages are some suggestions for you to review.

FIND A MEDICAL SPECIALIST

There are medical professionals specially equipped to deal with infertility and high risk pregnancies. I highly recommend that you interview prospective doctors. Any doctor who is unwilling or too busy to grant you an interview, is too busy to provide you with the kind of care you desire. Another excellent way to find a good specialist is to get recommendations from people whom you know. Make sure they can heartily endorse the doctor and find out if their experience was successful in conceiving and delivering a baby. You may also want to call a university with a teaching hospital and ask for a recommendation. One client of mine saw three infertility specialists over the course of two years before she attended a seminar on infertility at a local hospital. She was so impressed with the doctor who gave the presentation that she became his patient. Within three months, she was pregnant! (Nine months later she delivered a healthy baby.) The other so-called specialists she had seen had never suggested that her husband's sperm be tested. Apparently, both she and her husband had reproductive problems that contributed to their fertility difficulties. Be aware that not all "specialists" are equal! Be bold and assertive with your questions as you search for the right doctor for your needs. No one will care as much about your next pregnancy as you!

JOIN A SUPPORT GROUP

Support groups can offer both emotional support and ideas about how other parents have coped with their loss. Additionally, you can share information about new medical advances and perhaps get a referral to an understanding and competent physician from a fellow group member. In our Empty Arms group, I have watched deep and lasting friendships form from the common bond of losing a child. Long after the group has ended these new found friends have kept in touch to support and pray for one another (and to attend an occasional baby shower!)

READ

There are medical advances being made in the area of miscarriage prevention and high-risk pregnancies. Go to your local university library and read some of the medical journals. You can ask the librarian for assistance. Also, you may want to read some parenting magazines that offer a layman's interpretation of various medical research in this area.

SEEK PROFESSIONAL HELP

Sometimes when I speak about miscarriage and grief recovery, I am asked, "Since depression is a common and normal response to loss, how do you know when your depression is significant enough to warrant professional help?" The best indicator that you need to consider professional psychotherapy is if you have **persistent symptoms that interfere with your daily functioning** such as:

◆ severe depression (which can include any or all of the following...)

   ❖ crying
   ❖ anxiety
   ❖ lack of appetite or binge eating
   ❖ insomnia or a desire to sleep all the time
   ❖ nightmares
   ❖ lack of sexual desire or fear of sex

❖ lack of interest in activities which previously brought you fulfillment

Other symptoms that may or may not accompany depression, but also warrant professional help, include the following:

◆ debilitating guilt
◆ obsessive thoughts about the miscarriage
◆ excessive or inappropriate anger
◆ severe marital conflict

I realize that attending a counseling session can be a stressful and anxiety-producing experience. Even making the initial phone call to schedule an appointment usually causes a person's heart to beat a little faster than normal! Typically, it is not the way most couples would choose to spend their precious and limited evening time. And, unfortunately, to make the obstacle even more foreboding, for some people there can be a strong stigma attached to seeking professional help. There are people who think they have to be crazy or suicidal before they step into my office. Actually, the large majority of my clients are normal, sane people who just need some extra help coping with life stressors. When I see someone for grief couseling after a miscarriage, we spend an average of six to eight sessions together. We use the exercises in this book and the time in session to focus on the client's feelings, grief recovery process, and marital relationship. That's it. No head-shrinking. No weird stuff.

Chapter Fifteen

STARTING YOUR OWN SUPPORT GROUP

"Lean on me when you're not strong. I'll be your friend, I'll help you carry on."

— Bill Whithers

Several years ago when I founded the Empty Arms support group at my church, I wasn't sure what to expect. I knew only that I wished there had been a Christian support group for grieving parents when we had lost our first baby. Looking back, I can see how grieving alone and in isolation only intensified my pain and further confirmed my false belief that "nobody can understand the pain of my loss." Only after I started to talk about my miscarriage with others did I begin to experience true healing. I later discovered that there was a community support group in our area — but it had a formidable cost for two recently graduated doctoral students with huge student loans and, more importantly, it was not Christ-centered. I wanted a group that understood and respected my belief in God and my relationship with Jesus Christ. I wanted a group that would allow me to vent my anger at God without telling me, "I told you

so," and labeling my faith a "crutch." I truly do not know
how people cope with the pain of miscarriage, stillbirth,
or infant death without God and the hope He gives to
those who love Him. For me, part of that hope is the
promise of eternal life and the knowledge that my "dead"
children still live — in eternity with God!

Because I had a clear idea of what I did and did not
want in a miscarriage support group, and I had professional training and experience facilitating various types
of groups, I decided to develop my own group. Since its
inception in 1993, Empty Arms has been very well received by our church members and regular attenders and
also has been a wonderful outreach to the general community. There are several obstetricians and hospitals in
the area that make regular referrals to our group. It's a
great feeling to know our group has touched the lives of
other hurting parents. Many of these former group members have gone on to become trained group facilitators
for Empty Arms!

Perhaps you are one of those people with a compelling desire to use your own loss to help other people heal.
I sincerely believe that God gives us the chance to use our
painful experiences to help others and to strengthen our
relationship with Him. The Bible tells us this in many
ways, but one of my favorite passages is found in II
Corinthians 1:3-6..

> Praise be to the God and Father of our
> Lord Jesus Christ, the Father of compassion
> and the God of all comfort, who comforts
> us in all our troubles, so that we can com-
> fort those in any trouble with the comfort
> we ourselves have received from God. For
> just as the sufferings of Christ flow over into
> our lives, so also through Christ our com-
> fort overflows...

Through Empty Arms and my work as a psychotherapist, I have found a new depth of understanding concerning myself, others, and God as I share in the healing process of grieving parents. Never assume you are finished learning from your loss. God is always willing to teach us and I have discovered that the people I am helping are, in turn, helping me to grow and mature in my own life journey. If you feel that God has instilled in you a desire to be involved in an Empty Arms type of ministry, I encourage you to seek God's direction and guidance through prayer and counsel with trusted people who know you well.

Starting a support group involves hard work. But the good news is that we at Empty Arms have already done a great deal of it for you. We are eager to share our ideas and materials with anyone who is serious about starting a support group in his or her area (see appendices C-E). In fact, we have already approached several churches in the Southern California area, volunteering our time for training purposes. My dream is that this type of support group will someday be readily available throughout the country to help grieving Christian parents. It has been heart-wrenching for me to tell people who call me that I am unaware of a Christian-based support group like ours in their area. It has also been equally distressing to know that there are people in our own area needing and wanting help NOW, and they have to wait until we have enough people to start a new group. My goal is to have enough facilitators and available meeting room space to be able to start a new group every month in our area so that people have a minimal waiting period.

As you consider starting your own support group, I encourage you to choose your leaders carefully. In my opinion, the most important ingredient in making this type of support group a success is strong and mature leadership. Look for leaders with the following qualifications:

1. **Someone who has experienced a miscarriage, stillbirth, or infant death.** Why is this important? I have found this a necessary prerequisite to establish credibility with hurting parents. The common loss promotes bonding which, in turn, encourages a constructive discussion process within the group. Without this common loss, there is the likelihood that some group members will harbor lingering doubts about the group leader's ability to thoroughly understand and appreciate the depth of their pain. This may seem unfair (particularly if you know of someone who is very compassionate and understanding, but has not experienced this type of loss), however it does seem to be reality. Having a leader who has experienced a miscarriage is also helpful because the leader instills hope by providing a living role model of healing. Members begin to think, "Well, she had a really traumatic loss, but she got through it. If she can heal, then there is hope for my healing process." Because a leader has the potential to be a role model for hope and healing, it is also crucial that this person has worked through his or her grieving process before helping others. Occasionally, you may find people volunteering for leadership positions who have not truly addressed their own losses. Be prepared to address this issue and to aid such individuals to get the help they need before they accept leadership responsibilities.

2. **Someone with a heart for the Lord and a mature faith in God.** This is important for a number of reasons. Primarily a group leader must recognize the purpose of the group is to provide loving, non-judgmental support. It is not a place to preach or to evangelize aggressively. A group facilitator must be able to tolerate others' anger at God without feeling the need to defend God or chastise group members. And finally, a leader with a mature faith needs to know how to gently direct

(not force) members who are alienated from God towards a reconciliation with God.

3. **Someone with strong leadership skills.** I realize that leadership skills encompass a lot of different capabilities. Let me try to delineate the skills that I think are most helpful in running a ministry such as this.

a. Organizational skills — the ability to see the big picture, to break that picture down into a variety of tasks, and to delegate those tasks. (Empty Arms has a Ministry Coordinator position and a number of other positions as well. We have people who do not want to be facilitators, but deliver brochures to hospitals and doctors' offices, keep our lending library updated, make phone calls, write and mail our newsletter, and send out condolence cards and congratulation cards.)

b. Ability to listen well, summarize what others have said, and keep the group on track. (This is true whether one is leading a support group discussion or a steering committee meeting for the ministry.) The wonderful thing about working with groups is the energy that the members create together. Of course this energy can easily turn into chaos unless a leader is directing, redirecting, and focusing participants.

c. Diplomatic and skilled in coping with disagreements within the support group and/or the steering committee.

d. Recruits well and trains well. Not everyone is suited to be a group facilitator (even if he or she wants to be!). A Ministry leader/coordinator must be able to recognize someone's strengths and weaknesses and assign that individual a position for which he or she is well-matched.

e. Tolerates and considers constructive criticism from others. Also, one should know how to deal with criticism that is not particularly constructive. As I tell my group leaders, the negative feedback is part of the leadership package and it is important to model an appropriate way to deal with conflict.

f. Vision for the ministry — someone who is always looking for ways to improve things.

g. Genuine enthusiasm for the ministry. This type of energy is contagious!

4. **Someone who has experience facilitating small group discussions.** It is helpful to have someone with group facilitator experience because groups can be challenging to manage. The most common challenges are the silent member who refuses to talk or minimizes his or her pain (and by doing so, indirectly minimizes the pain of the other group members), and the group talker who monopolizes the discussion. Of course the **worst** thing that can happen to a support group is a *group leader that monopolizes the discussion!* There are other conditions that make group leadership challenging — some of which I am sure you will discover on your own! If you cannot find someone experienced with groups who meets all the other requirements, you may be able to find a professional counselor who is willing to train your group leaders so they feel prepared to handle the complexities that occur during group process.

As you begin your support group, be open to making changes and adjustments as you learn more about the needs of the people you will be serving. Through trial and error, we have made a number of changes and additions to our support group (we always ask for written and verbal feedback from group members at the last meeting, too!)

I would like to share with you some of the basic building blocks of our support group — what best suits our needs. Hopefully, these ideas will give you a foundation upon which you can tailor make a support group/ministry to meet your own needs.

1. **Length and duration of group** — We have discovered that an eight-week session works best for us. Our groups meet one evening a week for eight consecutive weeks. Each meeting is ninety minutes in length and we have a specific topic for the evening directly related to one (or more) of the chapters in this book to help focus and guide our members through the grieving process. (See Appendix C for a sample group schedule). We find that giving the group members some assigned reading and exercises outside of the group time helps prime the pump for the work we do in our group sessions. Members have already tapped into their feelings which means they arrive at our sessions emotionally acccssiblc. Secondly, we offer this type of topical structure to keep our group members focuscd and moving forward in their grief recovery process. Of course, we also allow for flexibility in our discussions.

2. **Size of group** — We try to keep our groups small and intimate (approximately twelve people, excluding the facilitator). We find that the smaller groups promote bonding and emotional intimacy. The larger the group, the more difficult it is to make sure everyone has adequate time to share and the more likely it is that you will have more than one challenging group member with whom to deal.

3. **Facilitators** — Typically I lead my groups alone, however, we have several facilitator teams. We like the results we get when husbands and wives team up to facilitate. It seems that other husbands who have just experienced a loss are more likely to attend a group if they are aware that one of the facilitators is a male.

4. **Always be prepared!** — As a facilitator you should have a list of competent, Christian, counselors, psychologists, psychiatrists, and obstetricians at your fingertips so that you can make a referral when necessary. If you are

unsure of when it is appropriate to make a referral, review the preceding chapter on Special Circumstances.
Undoubtedly, it is always much easier to give a referral
when a group member requests one. However, there will
be occasions when you will recognize a need and you will
be compelled to take the initiative. I recommend that
you talk with the group member individually and men-
tion your concern. You do not need to go into great detail about why you think a member needs help. It is best
to keep your referral discussion caring and short. The
conversation could go something like this:

> *You know, Susan, I've been wondering
> how you are doing these days. You seem
> especially sad and tearful in group. Some-
> times people find group really helpful but
> still not quite enough to get out of that very
> painful, dark place. Would you be interested
> in a referral to a counselor who specializes
> in grief recovery? We've had members in
> the past who have gone to see her for just a
> few sessions and they have found the extra
> one-on-one time very healing.*

Of course, you do not need to memorize this and re-
cite it as a speech. This is just an example of what you
might say. It is always important that whatever you say,
you allow for appropriate pauses and verbal interaction
with your group member. You don't want to overwhelm
someone with what may sound like a prepared mono-
logue. If Susan expresses any interest in the referral (this
includes a "maybe," "I don't know," or "I'll think about
it"), offer her the card or number. She can always hold
onto it until she needs it or discard it if she decides she is
not interested. If she says, "No thank you," then you need
to respect her right to make that decision and drop the

subject. If, however, Susan's special needs make trouble for the group process (such as dominating discussion time), you will need to address her particular troublesome behaviors and set appropriate boundaries with her.

5. **Get the word out!** — You want people to come to your group to get the help and healing you have to offer. If they don't know about it, they're going to miss a wonderful opportunity. One of the first things I did after starting our Empty Arms ministry was to write and design a brochure. We have found this to be a great tool to advertise our group. Our brochure describes common emotional reactions people suffer after a miscarriage, stillbirth, or infant death; it gives them hope that their pain can heal; it describes specifically what our ministry has to offer; and it gives facilitator profiles so potential group members know that each of us has overcome our own grief. We distribute these brochures to hospitals, doctors, and psychotherapists in our area. I am more than happy to send you a copy of our brochure and, if you find it suits your needs, you may adapt it to your particular circumstance and use it with my blessing.

6. **Telephone number** — Our Empty Arms ministry and support group actually has several different numbers. We started out using my professional voicemail number and a number at our church. I still receive occasional calls on my voicemail, but we now have a voicemail set up by the current ministry coordinator that is exclusively for Empty Arms. On this voicemail message we also have the phone number of our 24-hour hotline and the name of the contact person for people with urgent needs. We have found the voicemail system works well for us because we can receive a call and return it when we are able to talk freely. (Be prepared for long phone calls.) If you receive a phone call at **home** from a potential group member and she can tell from the background noise that you

have children or a baby, this can be very awkward and even painful for someone who has just lost a child. If your church fields the initial calls, valuable time can be lost as the message is relayed to you. In addition, we have found that when people call the church, they want specific information about the group (times, dates, structure, etc.) and they are hoping to speak with someone directly involved with the ministry. Typically, a church secretary or receptionist is answering the phone and may not be able to thoroughly address all the the caller's concerns.

People in pain and crisis do not want to make more than one phone call or be given partial information. It's hard enough for most people to make the first call. Whatever telephone system you use, be sure you return calls promptly and avoid shuffling people from one phone number to the next.

7. **Recruit and Delegate** — You cannot build and sustain this ministry alone because YOU WILL BURN OUT!! When a depleted leader trys to minister to the needs of others, everyone loses and that is definitely a development you want to avoid. Besides, this is the kind of ministry that begs for group involvement. Giving other people the opportunity to help you carry the responsibility of this ministry is a double blessing: You get relief and other people feel great when they can use their gifts to help others! There are a number of jobs within our ministry that are available to people with various aptitudes. As I said before, not everyone is a gifted facilitator, but Empty Arms uses people with other wonderful, God-given strengths to add flavor to our ministry. See Appendix D for a listing of our current job descriptions.

I hope that you have found this chapter useful and that it may prove to be a reliable blueprint as you begin to build your own support group ministry. I pray that you experience God's guidance in your endeavors. Again, I am willing to offer whatever support and advice I can. Feel free to write for more information:

Shari L. Bridgman, Ph.D.
c/o BlackHawk Canyon Publishers
25283 Cabot Road, Suite 204
Laguna Hills, CA 92653

Epilogue

There is a time for everything, and a season for every activity under heaven:

> a time to be born and a time to die,
> a time to plant and a time to uproot,
> a time to kill and a time to heal,
> a time to tear down and a time to build,
> a time to weep and a time to laugh,
> a time to mourn and a time to dance,
> a time to scatter stones and a time
>   to gather them,
> a time to embrace and a time to refrain,
> a time to search and a time to give up,
> a time to keep and a time to throw away,
> a time to tear and a time to mend,
> a time to be silent and a time to speak,
> a time to love and a time to hate,
> a time for war and a time for peace.

Ecclesiastes 3:1-8

As I relect on our life since August 1990 when we suffered our first miscarriage, I am reminded of the many seasons that Laird and I have experienced together. There have been times of great joy, contentment, and thankfulness. There also have been times of deep sorrow, tears, and tribulation. Through everything we have remained committed to each other and to our faith in God, and it is this commitment that has kept us moving forward during the worst of times.

Today as I sit here in front of my computer wondering how to finish a story which will continue even after this manuscript is finished, I am filled with a bittersweet feeling. Recently, Laird and I discovered that I was pregnant for the fifth time. As with my other pregnancies, apprehension and emotional guardedness became my constant companions. Although I desperately wanted to enjoy the miracle growing inside of me, I didn't want to allow myself to bond too early because what if....

Six short weeks into my pregnancy I began spotting and I knew in my heart that I was losing another baby. An ultrasound revealed that the embryo had not grown for two weeks and that, indeed, a miscarriage was imminent.

From a physical aspect, this was my easiest miscarriage (if one can ever really use "easy" to describe a miscarriage). Emotionally, I was still adjusting to the idea of another child and the pregnancy had not yet become fully "real" to me. Nevertheless, my heart still ached with emptiness and I still asked WHY? While I was prepared for the various emotions that accompany grief, a new and troubling feeling arrived with this loss: I felt defective.

Since this was my third miscarriage, I had become an official medical CASE. All of a sudden, previous losses that had been explained to me as random and rare (well, at least the second loss was considered rare) biological occurrences were now being categorized as a habitual miscarriage pattern that warranted investigation. My doctor recommended a blood panel analysis on me to rule out a variety of problematic medical conditions and genetics counseling to determine whether Laird and/or I had any chromosomal abnormalities that put us at risk. (Frankly, in my mind I believed that every pregnancy of mine involved risk.) Progesterone therapy from the time of ovulation through the twelfth week of pregnancy was encouraged for any future pregnancies. And of course, an amniocentesis would be inevitable. Wow! My head was reeling! I felt incredibly small and flawed. "Could there be something abnormal in me causing the deaths of my babies?" I wasn't sure I wanted to know the answer to such a question. I wasn't sure I could face the answer.

Our loss is still quite fresh and Laird and I are grappling with some important issues. "Do we try again? Should we just be thankful for our two healthy boys and avoid the possibility of any more heartache? If we do try again, do we follow the doctor's recommendations? Are they all necessary? What do you want, Lord?" Right now we do not have any answers. We are simply trying to cope with our grief, revisiting the lessons in this book.

The death of our third child brings us another sorrow-filled season. Yet, even our sadness is tempered by the wonderful joy we experience every time we look at our sons or hear their squeals of delight as they play together. What an awesome responsiblity — raising two boys to be all that God created them to be! Children truly are an incredible blessing from God and I thank Him daily for such precious gifts.

Jordan is now five and a half and he recently accepted Jesus Christ as Lord and Savior of his life. He is a bright, energetic, exuberant, intense, expressive, kind-hearted boy who loves to talk, and talk, and talk. He likes to putter around with his "inventions," ride his bike (without training wheels!), and tell knock-knock jokes with truly creative (if nonsensical) twists. His inquisitive mind is always trying to make sense of the world and he is continually asking questions such as: "Do angels' wings make noise when they flap?" and "Who created God?"

Carson is now two and a half and he is a sparkling, intelligent, energetic, loving, mischievous boy who also likes to talk, and talk, and talk! Daily, he warms our hearts with big kisses and his favorite question, "You know what? I love you so much." We covet our snuggle time with him and enjoy watching him fine-tune his future mountain climbing techniques by regularly scaling our kitchen cabinets. Alas, Carson is currently struggling with his human limitations as he has come to realize that he cannot fly.

Our two boys keep our hearts full and grateful even in the midst of the inevitable pain that life brings. Few things can compare to hearing Jordan tell his younger brother, "Carson, I love you to infinity, and that is much higher than you can count." or Carson declaring that "Jawah [Jordan] is my big brofer [brother] and best friend. He's a feetheart [sweetheart]." Yes, we feel extremely fortunate (particularly in light of our own losses and the fact that so many deserving people struggle with childlessness) and we gratefully remember Who is responsible for the blessings in our lives.

Every good and perfect gift is from above, coming down from the Father of the heavenly lights, who does not change like shifting shadows.

James 1:17

In His Love,

Shari Bridgman

Appendix A

SELF-HELP ORGANIZATIONS

Center for Sibling Loss
The Southern School
1456 W. Montrose
Chicago, IL 60613

CLIMB, Inc.
Center for Loss in Multiple Birth
PO Box 1064
Palmer, AK 99645
(907) 746-6123

The Compassionate Friends
PO Box 3696
Oakbrook, IL 60522-3696
(708) 990-0010

Empty Arms Support Group
Saddleback Valley Community Church
23456 Madero, Suite 100
Mission Viejo, CA 92691
(714) 581-9100 ext. 132 or (714) 491-4152

National Sudden Infant Death Syndrome Foundation

10500 Little Patuxent Parkway, Suite 420
Columbia, MD 21044
(301) 459-3388 Maryland
(800) 221-SIDS

Pregnancy and Infant Loss Center

1415 E. Wayzata Blvd.
Wayzata, MN 55391
(612) 473-9372

Resolve, Inc.

1310 Broadway
Somerville, MA 02144-1779

Resolve through Sharing Bereavement Services

Lutheran Hospital - La Crosse
1910 South Ave.
LaCrosse, WI 54601
(608) 791-4747

Share

St. Joseph Health Center
300 First Capitol Dr.
St. Charles, MO 63301
(314) 947-6164

St. Elizabeth's Hospital
211 South Third St.
Belleville, IL 62222
(618) 234-2415

**Contact your local hospital or obstetrician for additional support group recommendations.

Appendix B

BOOKS FOR CHILDREN COPING WITH GRIEF

AVAILABLE AT CHRISTIAN BOOKSTORES:

Death and Beyond, James Watkins (Teen)

Emma Says Goodbye, Carolyn Nystrom (elementary)

Heaven Is..., Linda DeYmaz (elementary)

My Mom Is Dying: A Child's Diary, Jill Westberg McNamara (elementary)

Someday We'll Play in Heaven, Shawn Alyne Strannigan (preschool)

Someone I Love Died, Christine Harder Tangvald (elementary)

What Happens When We Die?, Carolyn Nystrom (elementary)

AVAILABLE AT LOCAL BOOKSTORES:

A Funeral for Whiskers, Dr. Lawrence Balter
  (ages 3 -7)

Grover, Vera and Bill Cleaver (grades 4-6)

Helen the Fish, Virginia L. Kroll (elementary)

I Had a Friend Named Peter, Janice Cohn
  (ages 3-8)

I'll Always Love You, Hans Wilhelm (elementary)

Lifetimes, Bryan Mellonie & Robert Ingpen
  (ages 4-8)

Saying Good-bye to Daddy, Judith Vigna
  (elementary)

Straight Talk About Death for Teenagers, Earl A.
  Grollman (Teen)

Talking About Death, Earl A. Grollman
  (elementary)

The Girl Inside, Jeannette Eyerly (grades 5-9)

The Saddest Time, Norma Simon, (ages 6-12)

The Kids' Book about Death and Dying, Eric E.
  Rofes (elementary)

The Tenth Good Thing About Barney, Judith
  Viorst (elementary)

Appendix C

SUPPORT GROUP SESSION SCHEDULE

DATE	TOPIC
Session One	Introduction and Group Goals Review guidelines for sharing
Session Two	Sharing Experiences Chapters 1-3
Session Three	Feelings/The Grief Cycle Pregnant Again (apprehension) Chapters 3,6,7,13
Session Four	Husbands and Wives Chapter 4
Session Five	Dealing with Friends and Family Chapter 8
Session Six	Where is God? Chapters 5, 10
Session Seven	Saying Hello and Good-bye Balloon Ceremony Chapters 11, 12
Session Eight	Conclusion/Feedback Evaluations

Appendix D

MINISTRY
JOB DESCRIPTIONS

Ministry Coordinator: Oversees ministry. Schedules support group dates, recruits facilitators and other steering committee members, chairs quarterly ministry steering committee meetings, records minutes of meetings and distributes them to ministry steering members, purchases and distributes *In Heavenly Arms* for group members' use, keeps updated membership list with names, addresses, and phone numbers.

Facilitator Training Coordinator: Trains new facilitators using Facilitator's Guide. Makes sure that new recruits are adequately prepared for the job, reports any training or personnel difficulties to Ministry Coordinator (This job may be subsumed under the Ministry Coordinator if necessary).

Facilitator: Facilitates support group discussions, makes referrals to professionals when appropriate, attends steering committee meetings, phones group members on a regular basis, delivers a group roster including names, addresses, and phone numbers to Ministry Coordinator, makes *In Heavenly Arms* available to group members, collects written evaluations at end of group, reports any feedback or suggested changes in group operation or ministry operation at steering committee meetings, makes lending library and Scrapbook of Miracles available to group members at each session.

24-Hour Support Person: Carries a pager with voicemail, available 24-hours a day to return crisis and urgent phone calls from people who have suffered a miscarriage, stillbirth, or infant death. Activates prayer chain when desired by caller.

Outreach Coordinator: Shares support group idea and information with other churches, distributes brochures to hospitals, medical doctors, psychologists, psychiatrists, social workers, and marriage, family, child counselors. Tracks all outreach efforts.

Caring Heart Coordinator: Sends condolence (members who have had another loss) and congratulation (members who have new baby) cards, sends "thinking of you" cards at anniversary of loss, plans baby showers and support group reunions, creates and updates ministry's "Scrapbook of Miracles" (photo album with pictures of group members and their babies) as a tangible reminder that there is hope!

Prayer Chain Coordinator: Organizes and oversees prayer chain.

Newsletter Editor: Writes, organizes, and edits quarterly newsletter for former and current support group members. Solicits news from ministry steering committee and support group members. Maintains a current membership list and mails newsletter.

Librarian: Creates, updates, and organizes Lending Library. Solicits donations of books or articles from group members, makes Library available to current group facilitator for group use.

GUIDELINES FOR GROUP SHARING

DO...

...share the important details of your miscarriage.

...share your feelings.

...respect time (others need to share, too).

...listen empathically. Use your nonverbal skills to communicate caring and concern.

DO NOT...

...criticize or judge another person's experience or feelings.

...try to say the "right thing" or feel responsible for alleviating someone else's pain.

...ask a lot of questions of another member when he or she is sharing.

...interrupt the person who is sharing.

REMEMBER...

...everything that is shared in your small group is CONFIDENTIAL. Please respect each other's privacy and leave shared information in this room.

Appendix F

INTERNET RESOURCES

Information regarding miscarriages, medical testing, infertility, and support groups is now available through a variety of websites. Currently, you can find grief support and answers to your medical questions in the convenience and privacy of your own home. Here are some suggestions:

MISCARRIAGE INFORMATION
AND GRIEF SUPPORT

* Dealing with the emotional aspects of miscarriage

> http://www.resolve.org/friedman.htm
> Rochelle Friedman, M.D.

* D.E.S. information page

> http://www.geocities.com/HotSprings/2510/
> info.html

*For people with questions about D.E.S. and its link
to miscarriages and infertility*

* For parents who have suffered miscarriage

> http://www.ivf.com/misc.html

* Grief, loss of child, and recovery

> http://pages.prodigy.com/gifts/grief2.htm

* Houston's Aid in Neonatal Death (H.A.N.D.)

  http://member.aol.com/handinfo1/
  handhome.html

* Hannah's Prayer (Christian support)

  http://www.quiknet.com/~hannahs/

* Hygeia™ - Pregnancy and loss

  http://www.connix.com/~hygeia/
  Michael R. Berman, M.D.

* Misc.Kids

  http://scalos.mc.duke.edu/~brook006/
  miscarriage.html

* Pen-Parents Inc. For parents who have lost a child of any age

  http://pages.prodigy.com/NV/fgck08a/
  PenParents.html

* Personal stories of loss

  http://wdg.mc.duke.edu/~brook006/stories.html

* RESOLVE (support for grieving parents)

  http://www.resolve.org/

* SANDS (Stillbirth and Neonatal Death Support)

  http://www.yarra.vicnet.net.au/~sands/
  sands.htm

* The Miscarriage Manual

  http://www.inciid.org/msmanl.html

* The miscarriage page

  http://teramonger.com/dwan/html/
  Miscpage.htm

* Turner's Syndrome

    http://www.eden.com/~ploof/Turners/

Discusses Turner's Syndrome, a female-linked disorder and its relationship to miscarriage.

* Why did I have a miscarriage?

    http://dspace.dial.pipex.com/town/parade/
    abc53/miscarr.htm

INFERTILITY AND
POST-MISCARRIAGE TESTING

* INCIID (International Council on Infertility Information Dissemination)

    http://www.inciid.org/

* Pregnancy loss evaluation services

    http://www.centerforhumanreprod.com/ples/
    ples.html

* Recurrent pregnancy loss and implantation failure program

    http://www.givf.com/immune1.html
    (that's the number "1" after "immune")

* Recurrent pregnancy loss testing

    http://www.pinelandpress.com/support/
    rpl.html

PREGNANCY AFTER A LOSS

* Pregnancy after miscarriage (PAM)

> Support available by sending e-mail request to
> pam.request@fensende.com

* Subsequent pregnancy after loss support (SPALS)

> Support available by sending e-mail request to
> SPALS-request@inforamp.net

* SPALS information

> http://www.inforamp.net/~bfo/spals.html

BIBLIOGRAPHY

Bergren, Wendy, *Mom is Very Sick—Here's How to Help.* Arcadia, CA: Focus on the Family Publications, 1982.

Borg, Susan and Lasker, Judith, *When Pregnancy Fails: Families Coping With Miscarriage, Stillbirth, and Infant Death.* New York: Bantam Books, 1981.

Cadoff, Jennifer, "Can We Prevent SIDS?" *Parents Magazine.* August, 1995.

Clayman, Charles, MD (Editor), *The American Medical Association Encyclopedia of Medicine.* New York: Random House, 1989.

Damico, David, *The Faces of Rage.* Colorado Springs: Navpress, 1992.

Frankl, Viktor, *Man's Search for Meaning.* Pocket Books, 1988.

Hagar, Laura, "Pregnancy After Miscarriage." *Parenting Magazine.* February 1995.

Katz, Lillian G., "Death in the Family." *Parents Magazine.* May 1991.

Kübler-Ross, Elizabeth, *On Death and Dying.* New York: Macmillan Publishing Company, Inc., 1969.

Lester, Andrew D., *Coping With Your Anger: A Christian Guide.* Philadelphia: The Westminster Press, 1983.

Lewis, C.S., *A Grief Observed.* New York: Bantam Books, 1980.

Lewis, C.S., *The Magician's Nephew.* New York: Collier Books, 1970.

Lyons, Beverly, "A Toddler's Grief." *Parents Magazine,* November, 1995.

Rank, Maureen, *Free to Grieve.* Bethany House, 1985.

Rubin, Theodore Isaac, *The Angry Book.* New York: Collier Books, 1969.

Salmon, Dena K., "Coping With Miscarriage." *Parents Magazine,* May, 1991.

Simkin, Penny, Whalley, Janet, and Keppler, Ann, *Pregnancy, Childbirth, and the Newborn: A Complete Guide for Expectant Parents.* Deephaven, MN: Meadowbrook, Inc., 1984.

Viorst, Judith, *Necessary Losses.* New York: Ballantine Books, 1986.

Vredevelt, Pam W., *Empty Arms.* Portland: Multnomah Press, 1984.

Worden, J. William., *Grief Counseling and Grief Therapy: A Handbook for the Mental Health Practitioner.* Springer Publishing Company, Inc., 1982.

Yancey, Philip, *Where Is God When It Hurts?* Grand
Rapids: Zondervan Books, 1977.

About the Author

Dr. Shari L. Bridgman

Dr. Bridgman is a licensed Marriage, Family, Child Counselor practicing in Laguna Hills, California. After completing her undergraduate degree at Wheaton College in Illinois, Dr. Bridgman earned both a Masters and Doctoral degree in Clinical Psychology from Biola University in La Mirada, California. She speaks on a variety of women's issues and has been a featured guest on local radio and cable television programs. In 1993, Dr. Bridgman founded the Empty Arms support group ministry at Saddleback Valley Community Church in Lake Forest, California. As a result of her personal and professional experiences, Dr. Bridgman has a special burden for grieving parents who have lost their babies through miscarriage. She and her husband, Laird, have suffered three miscarriages and have two surviving children, Jordan and Carson.

Notes

Notes

Notes

Notes

Notes

Notes

Notes

Order Form

To order additional books, please fill out the information below and return or fax to:

> BlackHawk Canyon Publishers
> 25283 Cabot Road, Suite 204
> Laguna Hills, CA 92653
> FAX 714-770-5433

Please make checks payable to:

> BlackHawk Canyon Publishers

A 10% discount is available on orders of 10 or more.

DATE OF ORDER			
NAME:			
ADDRESS:			
CITY/STATE			ZIP
PAYMENT METHOD	CHECK ○ MO/PO ○ CREDIT CARD ○		
EXPIRATION DATE:	CREDIT CARD TYPE: VISA ○ MC ○ AMEX ○		
CREDIT CARD NUMBER:			
AUTHORIZED SIGNATURE:			
SHIP TO:			
NAME			
ADDRESS			
CITY/STATE			ZIP

ITEM	NUMBER OF COPIES	PRICE	SUB-TOTAL
IN HEAVENLY ARMS		X $12.95	
CA RESIDENTS ADD 7.75% SALES TAX			
SHIPPING/HANDLING $1.85 FIRST BOOK .85 EA ADDITIONAL			
TOTAL			

Order Form

To order additional books, please fill out the information below and return or fax to:

      BlackHawk Canyon Publishers
      25283 Cabot Road, Suite 204
      Laguna Hills, CA 92653
      FAX 714-770-5433

Please make checks payable to:

      BlackHawk Canyon Publishers

A 10% discount is available on orders of 10 or more.

DATE OF ORDER	
NAME:	
ADDRESS:	
CITY/STATE	**ZIP**
PAYMENT METHOD	CHECK ○ MO/PO ○ CREDIT CARD ○
EXPIRATION DATE:	CREDIT CARD TYPE: VISA ○ MC ○ AMEX ○
CREDIT CARD NUMBER:	
AUTHORIZED SIGNATURE:	
SHIP TO:	
NAME	
ADDRESS	
CITY/STATE	**ZIP**

ITEM	NUMBER OF COPIES	PRICE	SUB-TOTAL
IN HEAVENLY ARMS		X $12.95	
CA RESIDENTS ADD 7.75% SALES TAX			
SHIPPING/HANDLING $1.85 FIRST BOOK .85 EA ADDITIONAL			
		TOTAL	